imageworks for men

BY THE SAME AUTHOR:

ImageWorks for Women
Surviving the Media

diana mather

imageworks for men

Thorsons
An Imprint of HarperCollins*Publishers*

Thorsons
An Imprint of HarperCollins*Publishers*
77–85 Fulham Palace Road,
Hammersmith, London W6 8JB

1160 Battery Street,
San Francisco, California 94111–1213

Published by Thorsons 1996

1 3 5 7 9 10 8 6 4 2

A catalogue record for this book is available from the British Library

ISBN 0 7225 3204 0

Printed and bound in Great Britain by
Caledonian International Book Manufacturing Ltd, Glasgow

To Oliver, who creates his own image.

To Peter and my partners in Public Image for all their help and support.

contents

acknowledgements

Peter Wheeler	Broadcaster, partner in Public Image
Charlotte Howard	Fox Howard, my agent
Jane Graham-Maw	Editor at large, Thorsons
Giles Brandreth	MP
John Fifield	Chairman, Fifield Glyn, Chartered Surveyors
Gerald McGregor	Tack Training Worldwide
Sheena Storah	Physiotherapist
Charles Grimaldi	Director of Corporate Affairs, Rentokil
Midland Holiday Inn Hotel	Manchester
Leslie Spears	Chairman, John Paul Mitchell Systems (UK) Ltd.
Rita Rowe	Joint Managing Director, Mason Williams PR
Jennifer Saunders	Actress and writer
Penny Junor	Journalist and broadcaster
James Leith	Writer and man of many talents
Colin McBain	Butler, Burghley House
David Williams	Managing Director, Emerging Markets Search and Selection Ltd.
David Thomas	Head of Development and Training Supply, BT
Hugh Smith	Graduate Entry, BT

Linsey Perry	Graduate Recruitment, BT
Ian Brown	Assistant Managing Director, NWS Bank PLC
George Dearsley	Journalist
Helen Sharman	Astronaut
Sarah Wetherall	Consultant and partner in Public Image
Delia Corrie	Actress and partner in Public Image
Mary Spillane	Founder, CMB
Leigh Bruce	Head of Corporate Communications, Saloman Bros
Claire Hill	Senior Lecturer in Human Resources Management, Anglia University
Will Whitehorn	Corporate Affairs Director, Virgin Group
Dr John Viney	Chairman, Hiedric and Struggles Ltd.
Lana Jeffers	Managing Director, Middleton Jeffers Recruitment Ltd.
Rebecca Hooper	Hooper's Shoes
Sue Wheeler	Personnel Officer, Network Productions, BBC North
John Walkley	Organisation and Manpower Development Manager, Royal Insurance
Janet Brown	Graduate Recruitment, Royal Insurance
Tim Sands (Jamie)	Senior stylist, New Wave, Altrincham
Geoff Hackett	Television Producer, Executive Business Channel
Duncan Miller	Lecturer in Media Studies, Redbridge College
Mark Borkowski	Chairman, Mark Borkowski PR
Sian Richards	Freelance make-up artist and television presenter
Arthur Andersen	Accountants
Natalie Anglesey	Broadcaster and presenter on London Radio
Simon Whittam	Publicist
Leila Potter	Managing Director, Bunbury Domestic and Equestrian Agency
Robin Wood	Chief Executive, Career Movers' Companion
Sue Hardy	Guardian Ad Litem
Clifford Merriman	Finance Director, Executive Standby Limited
Jeannie France-Hayhurst	Barrister
Jane Bibby	Marketing and design consultant
Leslie Phillips	Actor

Lenny Henry	Actor and comedian
Christopher Denton	Friend
Richard Thorpe	Actor
Michele Turney	Managing Editor, Thorsons

introduction

What is the right image, and why is it important? We all have an idea of how we project ourselves, but how many of us stand back and analyse the impression we convey to others? When we meet someone for the first time, ninety per cent of our opinion of that person will be formed within the first twenty to thirty seconds. If we want to project the right image, then, we do not have much time to waste.

We are naturally attracted to people who are similar to ourselves, a bit like an animal recognizing friend or foe by the colour of its fur or the smell of its skin. While we do not usually go round sniffing each other, the subconscious mind is very powerful. The way someone dresses, speaks, walks and eats all helps us to build a picture of that person. Clothes can tell us a lot about someone's lifestyle, giving pointers to his or her sort of job, salary and background. There are some people who are either so rich, so successful or so eccentric that the sort of image they project really does not matter, to them or anybody else. Most of us, however, have to take note of the way the world perceives us.

I am a partner in Public Image, a company that specializes in self-presentation, confidence building, motivation and personal communication, as well as advising on how to deal with the media. Founded twelve years ago, it became well known when cameras were introduced into the House of

Commons and MPs approached us to help them improve their image. During those twelve years I have had dealings with hundreds of people from all walks of life. I have worked for organizations both large and small as well as for individuals wanting to 'change their image'.

Before joining Public Image I trained as an actress and singer, gaining invaluable experience in self-expression and voice control. After reading the news for BBC North for nearly ten years, I am now a presenter for the Executive Business Channel. This involves interviewing men and women who might be running their own businesses or have become the chief executives of multinational corporations. This combination of broadcasting and consultancy experience puts me in an ideal position to know what goes into creating and maintaining a positive image.

Is it feasible to create an image? Of course it is, but your image should mirror your personality as much as possible. A drastic change should not be necessary, perhaps just some fine-tuning. A positive image should transmit confidence, competence, reassurance and responsibility. It means being prepared for any situation by doing your homework. It means knowing your strengths and weaknesses, as well as dressing with style and care. Image must be based on reality, so if you are sure in your own mind who you are, what you are good at and where you are going, you will automatically portray a positive image. Let us examine what goes into forming that image.

YOUR CLOTHES

Some of us have a different image for home and work. I am a casual dresser by nature, and am happiest in jeans or leggings coupled with long T-shirts or sweaters, but when I dress up I like to wear something that will get me noticed! I have learned, however, that while this might have been fine when I was an actress, my current job demands a high standard of dress. I still wear what I like when at home (especially when I am writing) or on holiday, but for work I have to present a positive image.

In the past, people had more stereotyped images than they do today. A fishmonger donned a striped apron, a travelling salesman could afford only a cheap suit, a farm labourer wore a smock and an artist sported a beard and long hair. Choosing clothes to create a positive image takes time but not necessarily too much money, as high-street shops provide some really smart clothes at affordable prices. It is, however, a good plan to save up and buy well-made clothes that will mix and match rather than lots of cheap ones. A smart jacket, well-cut trousers and some good shoes will never let you down. As you grow older, clothes need to be of a better fit and quality. You can get away with more when you are young. If you buy an expensive suit that fits really well, you know you look good, which gives you a huge amount of confidence.

It goes without saying that cleanliness is fundamental. Always check your clothes for marks or creases before wearing them, and keep your shoes polished. These days the barriers in both career and class terms are breaking down, but there are still certain rules that should be obeyed. Do not worry – all will be revealed as you read on!

YOUR BODY

These days, an important part of a positive image is to appear physically fit and mentally alert, especially in the workplace. The working environment is increasingly competitive, and there is a trend at present for one person to do the work of at least two people. So it is essential to look as though we will be able to stand the strain and cope with the workload. Our personal lives are often just as demanding as we try to fit more and more into what may already be a hectic lifestyle.

Take the thorny issue of weight. A seriously overweight person sends out certain signals. To some, it says 'this person is lazy and probably rather idle; his body is out of control and so is his mind'. To others, it might say 'this person is obviously stable and secure in himself' although, unfortunately, that is less likely. The problem is that you do not know the effect your image is going to have, so it is best to steer a middle course where possible. That does not mean going on a crash diet and changing fundamentally, but polishing up the rough edges.

Not many of us are completely happy with our image, but there are many things we can do to promote a healthy, professional and positive image without necessarily striving for perfection. A nutritious diet and sensible exercise routine is essential to keep us looking good, as is enough sleep; but too often lunch breaks slip by, a burger fills that gap and a couple of pints or large glasses of vino help to ease the stress of another long day. Looking pale and pasty does not earn promotion, so in Chapter 1 I will be giving some tips on how to repair the ravages of too little sleep, too much junk food and not enough exercise.

YOUR MIND

A positive image starts the minute you get up in the morning, and it is as much a matter of attitude as anything else. The way you react to other people builds up an image in their mind. Try and think of the effect your actions and reactions will have on others. Show that you care, not only about yourself, but about others too. We are all human beings living in society together, and life is a compromise. We have to show respect for others, which in turn brings respect for ourselves. In the cut and thrust of today's working environment, the pressure to perform can outweigh the natural courtesies of reasonable behaviour. The emphasis on winning at all costs can turn rational, moderate human beings into monsters. Honesty and integrity should be part of any long-term business strategy and culture, otherwise success will be perfunc-tory and short-lived. Sincere, straightforward communications are essential because, however strong your message is, it is lost if you cannot get it across. Help is at hand, however, in Chapter 6.

How do you 'broaden the mind'? Newspapers and magazines can play a significant part in expanding horizons. It is not easy to converse on any level if you read only the tabloids and *What Car?* magazine. Reading one of the serious broadsheet newspapers at least once a week, as well as magazines such as *Time* or *The Spectator*, keeps you informed of world opinion and events. Nobody expects you to be a political analyst or an expert on the economy, but if you are among a group of people and cannot contribute sensibly to a discussion, it does not do much to enhance a public image!

YOUR VOICE

'It is not what you say, but the way that you say it' that makes people remember and take notice. The way we use our voice is meaningful if we want to make a good impression. Accents are not as significant as they used to be, but they obviously pinpoint where we come from or where we were brought up, and it is as well to be aware that some accents arouse in-built prejudices.

To many southerners, anything that sounds north of Watford immediately evokes the North–South divide. A strong Liverpool or cockney accent could raise doubts about honesty and trustworthiness, and a very plummy accent might be taken as indicating a lack of intelligence and common sense. I am not suggesting that you should necessarily change the way you speak, but it is essential to be aware of the impression you are giving.

If, for example, you have a very pronounced Liverpool inflection and want to do business with someone from Hampshire, whose only image of Liverpool has been formed by watching *Brookside*, do not dress in a sharp suit. Choose something in a sober colour with a classic cut. This will immediately give the impression of somebody who is confident, competent and reliable.

The most important thing is to be understood wherever you are, and that means speaking clearly and audibly. More on that in Chapter 3.

YOUR FACE

As I have already said, people's first impressions are made on how we look, whether we like it or not, and we ignore that fact at our peril. Obviously, ability is what matters most, but if you are representing your organization you must reflect its image. When you stand in front of the mirror what do you see? Most of us are taught that it is vain to spend too much time looking at ourselves, and that self-analysis is only for psychology students. Of course, to spend the day contemplating our navel, or anything else for that matter, would not do us or anyone else any good; but it is important to evaluate our strengths and weaknesses so that we can 'maximize the positive and minimize the negative'. A smile, for instance, will not only influence how someone reacts to you face to face, but it will also warm
your voice when using the telephone.

YOUR HAIR

Hair projects an immediate image. If a man is bald or prematurely grey, he will probably look older than his years. If he has long, dark, flowing locks, he will look younger, and so on. Your hair can also say whether you are healthy or not and how much you care about your appearance. A good haircut can transform a face and completely alter an image.

STYLE

What makes somebody 'stylish'? Good grooming is essential, of course, but being stylish does not necessarily mean wearing expensive clothes. Rather, it is the overall image of being smartly, appropriately presented in an often understated way. Which men in the public eye do you consider stylish? Thirty years ago, Cary Grant, Sean Connery and David Niven were considered the epitome of style, but today 'style' has changed. The more affluent the society, the more it tends to dress down.

Whether you own a fortune or spend one, you cannot buy style. Having style means wearing clothes that fit really well; it means wearing something that little bit different (whether it is a hand-made shirt, an unusual tie or T-shirt or perhaps an amazing pair of boots); it means thinking about yourself and your image; it means taking time.

I suppose it is the sad truth that real style is something we are born with. Think of the people who stand out among your friends. What is it that gets them noticed? In Chapters 1 and 2 there are some tips to help you develop your own style.

CONFIDENCE

A lot goes into building an image, and being confident as well as competent are two of the main ingredients. So how can you gain the confidence needed to make an impact and get that job, secure a long-awaited promotion or make friends and influence people? As I said, first of all you have to take a long, hard look at yourself. It can be a painful process as no one likes to admit their shortcomings, but admit them we must if we are going to project the positive image that is a requirement in today's competitive world. You should not wear a suit if you are not used to wearing one, but anyone can wash and brush his hair and put on a clean pair of jeans!

Everybody has positive points on which to build, although it may not be immediately obvious to you what they are. For instance, if you were the eldest child of working parents, and have had to look after younger siblings, you most probably have an in-built sense of responsibility that could be valuable for any job in a supervisory capacity. Dealing with cantankerous, ageing relatives also enables you to cope with difficult customers. But how many of you would think of mentioning this on your CV? Holiday jobs and travel experiences are important when it comes to adding up positive achievements and experiences. If you can drive, cook, use a word processor, speak a foreign language, spell correctly or are good with figures, then you can start to build up a list of the things that will help you create a positive image of yourself. It may sound trivial, but everybody has something to offer.

Naturally, academic achievements are important, but for many jobs the employer is looking for something more, so think of something that will give added value and make you stand out from the rest. This need not necessarily be any great feat like climbing Ben Nevis or hang-gliding from the top of Blackpool Tower, but the fact that you can type, even though the job might not actually require this particular skill, may sway a decision in your favour. Chapter 4 will give you guidance you may be looking for.

SELF-IMAGE

But what *is* your image? Our idea of ourselves stems from early childhood and from the different events that happen to us as we grow up. Some things have a positive effect, such as a supportive family, doing well at school or excelling in sport. Our ability to communicate with other people also influences our self-image. Other factors in our development can diminish the positive image that most of us are born with. These include the loss of a parent, experiencing abuse, having parents who divorce, moving house a number of times or changing schools.

Whether your self-image be that of a salesperson, student, actor, singer or professional man – to name just a few examples – the important thing is to be happy with it. I cannot stress enough that, to succeed in life, we need to have a positive self-image, and in this book I will be concentrating on what we can do to boost it, especially in the workplace. If you feel you have a deep-seated problem, I would advise you to seek help from the specialist books and counselling services available. Once a problem is faced, it is well on the way to being solved.

YOUR SOCIAL IMAGE

People put us into categories when we say what we do. A man who dresses in a fairly conservative manner and says he is an accountant takes nobody by surprise. He might, however, if he were wearing beads and a kaftan.

The image we portray socially is often quite different from the one we depict at work. In certain circumstances, however, the image you create in the workplace should stay with you; if you are 'the Boss' then you cannot afford to let your hair down completely at the office party. But even at other social engagements it is quite possible to tarnish your image. In these days of upward mobility, many people are swept into sections of society where a particular code of conduct or dress is expected. It is impossible to feel comfortable if you are the only person in a suit when every other man in the room is wearing a dinner jacket. It can also be daunting when confronted by an intimidating row of cutlery!

What about public speaking? That is something very few of us look forward to, but whether it is speaking at a wedding or addressing the Rotary Club, presenting a positive image on the rostrum is crucial. Chapter 6 will allay all your fears.

YOUR PROFESSIONAL IMAGE

The way you present yourself professionally is the key to success. There are many things that can make you stand out, from what you wear to how you set out your CV, handle an interview or address an audience. Again, the image you create can be negative or positive. The car you drive says a lot about you, but even if you can only afford an old car, it will give you a positive image provided it is clean, well polished and tidy. Shoes and clothes should also be shining and pressed, and a well-organized briefcase is important too. And remember that an image has to be maintained once you have taken the trouble to build it up – an image can be broken in the pub, for instance, if drink loosens the tongue. But do not despair. All these things will be looked at in greater detail later.

If you run your own company or manage a department in a large organization, your image should have something in common with that of the majority of people who work there. When the law changed a few years ago to allow the legal profession to advertise, a young solicitor who had just set up a practice rang his local weekly newspaper and asked if they would like to do an interview with him and take his picture in the new office. The paper's initial answer was no. After all, new solicitors' offices open every day all over the country. However, this story was a bit unusual because there was going to be a kissogram girl on the premises. As kissograms were fairly new at the time, the paper sent a journalist round there like a shot! The solicitor got a half-page photo of a girl in lacy underwear and the interview that he had been looking for, saving himself hundreds of pounds in advertising.

That sort of publicity can be a double-edged sword, though. What was the image being projected? Potential clients who needed a solicitor to draft a will for their dying granny might have been put off. Some people, on the other hand, might have been impressed by the flair and imagination of a solicitor blowing away the cobwebs of the legal profession.

How can a company change its image? Rentokil is a recent success story. A decade or so ago, the name Rentokil brought to mind an image of scruffy ratcatchers. That has now changed to one of consistent, high-quality service. Over the last few years, Rentokil has been voted 'UK Company of the Year' and 'Best British Service Company in Europe', among other awards, all of which help to build a positive image, both inside and outside the company.

Rentokil invested their marketing budget in recruitment, training and communication skills, rather than creating the image through advertising. Charles Grimaldi, Director of Corporate Affairs, told me, 'If you work in tatty, scruffy premises and dress as though you do, you are more likely to under-perform than if you dress to a high standard. All those things help to consciously and subconsciously project a positive image.' I chose Rentokil recently to carry out some work at my house. I got several quotes, but Rentokil got the job because the representative turned up on time, wore a suit (even though he had to clamber up into the loft) and had all the relevant information to hand. The other firm I asked to come out and look at my house sent somebody who was wearing a smelly old anorak, gave me some rather dog-eared pieces of paper and did not really seem bothered whether he got the job or not. Added to that, the quotes were similar, so there was no contest!

In Chapter 4 you will find out about careers and what companies are looking for today.

CREATING AN IMAGE

Your image should be a positive thing that will help you succeed, but if it becomes too much of a trademark, it can be a millstone round your neck. Take the case of the actor Leslie Phillips. He told me that he has had many changes of image over the years. Originally, he had not particularly wanted to go on the stage, but thought it would be a good way to earn some money. His image developed when he was in his late twenties. Before that, he was like any other actor and played a range of parts. 'The only good thing about having a particular image is that people know who to come to for a particular part, which means you are a success,' he told me. 'In that sense you can't knock it. I had a tremendous following and people used to model themselves on me. Mark Jones, the doctor on *Good Morning*, actually told me on the air that he became a doctor because of me, and I said, "so that's what is wrong with the health service!" '

Leslie does not consciously keep up his screen image, but the fact that people want him to be the character they know means that he tends to project that image. He certainly likes women, which is one thing he shares with his screen persona!

Altering a successful image can be dangerous. Leslie had a slightly worrying time when he made up his mind to cut out the comedy and leave behind his traditional roles. 'I decided I didn't want to do them any more, up to the point that I would do anything rather than those parts again.' Over the years, however, he had done a number of different things, including writing and directing, so he was able to draw on this experience to change the public's perception of his image. Even so, it was a brave decision, as producers and directors did not take him seriously for quite some time. 'They thought that when I came on the screen or on stage that people would immediately laugh. But that is absolute rubbish – people only laugh if I want them to laugh, or if the part demands it.'

The biggest move Leslie had to make was to forget the 'star' thing and accept work that would help to change his image. He took cameo roles that were quite different to what we were used to as viewers, and once both the producers and the public got used to the change of image, the work and the better parts came flooding in. His cameo role in the film *Out of Africa* established him in Hollywood. 'People were surprised to see me. Even Prince Charles said, "What are you doing in this film? I haven't seen you in this kind of thing before" '. His appearance in a Chekhov play, *The Cherry Orchard*, at the Haymarket led to the part in *August* with Anthony Hopkins.

Another actor who has changed his image over the years is Richard Thorpe who plays Alan Turner, landlord of The Woolpack in *Emmerdale Farm*. He started his television career in the 1960s in *Emergency Ward 10*. His character, young Dr Rennie, was a heart-throb for many of the viewers.

Oxfam

08/07/2005 11:36   0001
000000#5151 CASHIER01

NON-FICT   *1.49

ITEMS   1Q
***TOTAL   *1.49
CASH   *1.50
CHANGE   *0.01

OXFAM [F1516]
18 CARTERGATE
NEWARK

Outside work, he was regularly mistaken for a doctor, as viewers were more naive in those days about the barriers between image and reality. He told me, 'If you were in a restaurant having a quiet meal, suddenly, from out of nowhere, about 400 people would appear at the window. I have been in several situations where I have been expected to give medical advice. The fact that I hate the sight of blood is neither here nor there – I had to keep up the image so that I didn't disappoint the fans.'

A lot of work goes into creating a successful image, and it is much easier to destroy it than to build it. Take the case of Shadow, the ex-Gladiator. He was caught using drugs while starring in a high-profile television programme, watched by millions of youngsters. The image of the clean-cut, responsible athlete was shattered, so the first thing Shadow had to do was hold his hands up and apologize. He had to try to revitalize his image, to be seen to be going straight, having cleaned up his act.

As the general public, we take vicarious pleasure in knocking down our heroes, but we are sympathetic and forgiving if we think someone is really trying to put things right. Just after the adverse publicity had broken, I accompanied Shadow to his appearance on BBC's *Good Morning*. I advised him that, instead of making excuses, he should take the blame fairly and squarely on his shoulders, which he did. Although the presenters gave him a hard time, the phone-in afterwards was very positive; the viewers were obviously prepared to give him a chance. But it is very difficult to start your life over again, and sometimes you are not given a second chance.

MAINTAINING THE IMAGE

Once you have created the right image, you have to maintain it, and that is not always as easy as it sounds. The following chapters look at ways of creating and maintaining the right image for you, whether it is to improve your chances of getting a job, enable you to make an impression on the social scene or just gain confidence generally. Whatever it is, I can only give you ideas and guidelines – your image must be you!

1

---

look good, feel good!

To look good you must feel good, so in this chapter we will look at clothes, exercise and diet.

CLOTHES

Clothes are the first thing other people notice about us. I have mentioned below just a few of the hundreds of designers and brands on the market, but I hope it will give you some idea as to where to start.

Body Shape

To know what suits you best, you need to be aware of your body type. Most men fit into one of the categories described below.

Triangular

Broad shoulders and narrow hips characterize this shape. You can wear most clothes, but you should avoid anything with very wide shoulders as this will make you look top heavy and rather intimidating. Trousers are best cut on the slim side and tightly woven fabrics suit you well.

Straight

If you are straight from shoulders to hips, looser, European-cut suits or jackets are best for you. Trousers should be of a slightly more generous nature, especially if you are at all broad in the beam.

Round

For men with a tummy, it is important to look as trim as possible, so do not choose very loose-fitting jackets except for weekend casual wear. Single-breasted suits are the most flattering unless you are really large, when an open double-breasted suit can hide a multitude of sins! Waistcoats look good too, as long as they do not make you feel too warm.

Pear

If you think that you could do with another couple of inches on your shoulders to balance the rest of you, a period of training sessions at the gym can work wonders. Otherwise choose a suit with defined shoulder pads to add substance, and trousers that are not too tailored.

Long Body, Short Legs

To make the most of your body type, buy jackets that reach your bottom and button high on the waist. Long, wide, low-buttoning jackets only draw attention to a long body, so the classic-tailored suit is by far the most flattering. Trousers should not be too wide, and avoid turn-ups as they can make the legs look shorter. Coats are better single-breasted, such as the chesterfield or greatcoat, and worn just below the knee.

Short Body, Long Legs

If you are on the thin side, it is best to steer clear of very tailored styles, and make sure that the jacket is long enough to balance your legs. Very narrow trousers can also exaggerate a flagpole appearance, so something with a bit of width is more flattering. Turn-ups are great for your shape if you favour them. If you want to make the most of your height, a single-breasted coat reaching almost to the ankles will certainly do the trick, but belted, double-breasted coats at mid-calf length are more classic.

Choosing a Suit

When buying a suit, it is often difficult to tell whether you are getting value for money. One thing is certain, however – the better the fabric, the more wear you will get from it. Whatever the price, make sure you choose natural fibres. Man-made cloth never breathes, hangs or lasts as well as wool or silk, and it never feels as comfortable. A well-made jacket should have no puckering where the shoulder meets the sleeve. Darts and patterns should line up meticulously and the garment must hang well. Test material by squeezing it to ensure that it is not going to crease too much, and if the item of clothing is light in colour, are you going to have to dry-clean it too often?

There are many different styles of suits and jackets. Once you have established your body shape, it is a good idea to try some on to see what suits you and which styles you prefer. Mary Spillane, the founder of image consultants CMB, gives excellent advice on colour and fit in her book *Presenting Yourself*. Indeed, if you are unsure which fabrics and styles are right for you, a session with an image-consultancy firm such as CMB or First Impressions is well worth the money. Both these firms employ consultants nationwide, and will give you confidential advice on what to wear and where to buy it. CMB can be contacted at 66 Abbey Business Centre, Ingate Place, London SW8 3NS. Write to First Impressions at The Coach House, Ramsey Manor, 37 High Street, Burwell CB5 0HD.

If you are only going to buy one suit, choose one that is cut on the narrow side, especially the trousers, as this style never really dates. A navy, single-breasted suit jacket will also double as a blazer to give you extra choice. A good suit must have some hand stitching if it is to fit really well. Collars, interfacing and sleeves should be hand-sewn to gain the best fit. Look underneath the collar – if the stitching is incredibly neat, then it has been done by a machine; if it is slightly uneven, it has been sewn by a tailor over a curved surface (his thigh) which makes the collar hang better over your curved neck.

Try separating the lining from the jacket, if you cannot, it has been glued together. After dry-cleaning the lining will start to pucker and you will not be able to press it straight, so the jacket will quickly lose its shape.

Double-breasted suits have between two and six buttons, four being the most classic. Single-breasted suits have between one and three buttons, with two being the most classic.

The British or Saville Row Suit

This tailored style follows the natural line of the body. The shoulders are only slightly padded and the waist is nipped in. The jacket usually has double vents at the back, and the pockets have a flap and are set slightly on an angle. The lapels are not too wide and the double-breasted version has four or six buttons.

The European Cut

Very padded shoulders have gone out with the 1980s, but this suit is still far less structured than its British counterpart, allowing more freedom of movement. The jackets are much longer and the trousers fuller, so it is best side-stepped by the shorter man. The jackets are buttoned low, with the double-breasted version having two to six buttons. Most of the jackets are ventless and the lapels are wider than the Saville Row suit. This cut is generally perceived to be more trendy.

The American Sack

This style has no extra padding on the shoulders, is much shorter than the European cut and is rather straight and 'boxy', defining neither the shoulders nor the waist. There is a centre vent and the pockets are flapped. This suit is marvellous for casual wear, especially for the larger man as it provides plenty of comfort. For business, however, it never looks really spruce or sharp.

The Fit

If you are going to spend hard-earned money on a decent suit, it is best to be measured by an experienced tailor. To take your own measurements, however, it is best to strip down to your underwear. Use the following guidelines:

Collar – put the tape measure around the base of your neck.
Chest – measure under the armpits and across the back, running the tape over the middle of your shoulder blades, not underneath them.
Sleeve – measure from the base of your neck, over the shoulder to the wrist bone.
Waist – draw the tape around your waistline, which should line up with your tummy-button.

Hips – measure round the widest part of your buttocks.
Inside leg – take the tape from the top of the inside leg to the ankle bone.

Colours

The old adage 'never brown in town' and tweed being suitable only for Fridays (because gentlemen were off to the country for the weekend) has faded now. However, the safest colours for suits are still blue and grey. This gives you more scope than you might think, as greys range from charcoal to very light grey, and blues from darkest navy to mid-blue. Before buying, try on suits in different colours until you find the most flattering for you.

Suit Jackets

Jackets should not strain across the shoulders, and lapels should lie smoothly on the chest when the buttons are fastened. There should be no pulling round the buttons (although this can easily be altered). When you stretch your arms there should be no pulling or straining, but no loose folds either. Sleeves should end at the wrist bone. If a suit jacket does not fit, there is no point even trying on the trousers as they will never look right.

Suit Trousers

Comfort in trousers is determined by the distance from crotch to waist, so try to match them as closely as possible to your measurements. The hemline should not be even all round, but about an inch or an inch and a half longer at the back. The trousers should fold back slightly on the top of the shoe, not swamping it or flapping round the ankles. The pockets should lie flat, even if you are carrying loose change or keys, and buttons or zips should never be strained. When buying suit trousers, walk round, sit and bend in them to make sure they are really comfortable.

A made-to-measure suit will cost anything from £1000 upwards. It is only really necessary to have a suit made if you have difficulty in buying off-the-peg. (Many men, however, aspire to having their suits made, as it gives them that extra 'something'.) Gieves and Hawkes will probably charge you that price for one of their top-of-the-range off-the-peg suits, and it would be difficult to tell the difference. The reason for the price is top-quality material, cutting and tailoring.

Austin Reed offers a range of high-quality business suits, not just the classic pinstripe for which the brand is best known. Jaeger Man is always a safe bet when choosing a quality suit. Suits from both these brands will cost between £350 and £450. Marks and Spencer, Burton and Next all stock what I would call 'everyday' suits – well made, but not as hard wearing as the more expensive brands. Next shops offer jackets and trousers as separates, which means you can buy two pairs of trousers with the jacket to extend the life of your suit. Burton was one of the first menswear companies to branch into mass-market retailing, and has years of experience in the field. Daks aims its stylish Studio Range mainly at the younger end of the market, with prices from around £199. Savoy Tailors Guild also provides a wide variety of styles and prices.

Suits by top designers tend to be more fashionable, less classic and less durable. Even Armani suits can date very quickly, so it is worth some thought before laying out anything from £350–£600 for a suit you might not wear for more than a year. Some designers, such as Yves Saint Laurent, license clothing manufacturers to produce items for them, and these suits tend to be the ones you see in department stores like Debenhams, House of Fraser and the John Lewis Partnership. Designs by Paul Smith, Boss and Pierre Balmain can also be found in these menswear departments.

Pockets

In her book *Presenting Yourself*, Mary Spillane gives the following useful guidelines about what can be carried in pockets without pushing the suit out of shape:

- Inside breast pocket – slim diary, notepad, calculator, envelope-style wallet, pen set.
- Outside breast pocket – only a handkerchief (preferably silk).
- Outside front pockets – business-card holder. Empty the pockets of any notes, receipts etc. each evening.
- Side trouser pockets – loose change, essential keys.
- Back trouser pockets – slim wallet if you are not wearing a jacket, but beware of pick-pockets!

Blazers and Jackets

A blazer will take you almost anywhere, so it is a good investment. A blue blazer looks good with grey trousers, or stone Chinos for the summer, as well as jeans for more casual wear. Prices start from £150. House of Fraser stock blazers that are very good value for money, including those under their brand name, Henry Fox. They will last at least a couple of years, even if worn frequently. Jaeger blazers are higher quality, but cost around £250. However, they will keep their good looks for longer, so it can be worth spending that bit more.

It is time to invest in a new blazer when shiny patches appear on the elbows, the lapels are limp and the jacket starts to look out of shape. Apart from a blazer, a black and white dogtooth or tweed jacket for the winter, and a lightweight wool-and-silk mixture for the summer are interesting and serviceable additions to your wardrobe. Again, prices start from £150.

Trousers and Jeans

A trouser press is a must if you want to keep trousers looking fresh and crisp. Good trousers will cost from £50. Tailored trousers should not be washed as they are usually made from a combination of cloths which dry and stretch at different rates, so dry-cleaning is the way to keep them in shape. The same criteria for choosing suits apply when shopping for trousers.

Moschino jeans are priced around £88, Calvin Klein jeans cost about £60 and Carhartt jeans start from £60. Levis can look just as smart as designer jeans, as it is the fit that counts. Shop around until you find a pair that fits comfortably and flatters you most. Once jeans become really faded, keep them for home use only. Most jeans are pre-shrunk these days, but even so, avoid washing or drying them at very high temperatures.

Coats

When buying a coat, it is a good idea to wear a suit so that you select the right size. Choose a classic style that will not date too quickly. In this country a mac or trench coat will be worn quite a lot, so be prepared to replace it every two years or so. As very few of them are really waterproof, it is worth spraying a mac or trench coat with Scotchguard before wearing, and again after dry-cleaning.

Shirts

Shirts come in all shades and prices, but natural fabrics are best, or a natural and man-made mix such as polycotton. There are different collar styles too, some purely fashionable, others more enduring. Choose one that flatters your features. Men with narrow necks and faces need wide collars to add balance, whereas men with fuller faces should wear narrow collars. To look right and be comfortable you should just be able to get one finger inside the collar.

A good shirt should lie with seams matching when you lay it down, and stripes on the pockets should be indistinguishable from those on the rest of the shirt. The more expensive shirts have a rounded pocket, if they have one at all, rather than one with a straight edge. These cost anything from £30 upwards. Van Heusen, Peter England and Vyella are all reasonable brands in terms of both price and quality, as are those sold by Marks and Spencer. For pure cotton and designer shirts you will pay more. Jaeger's start at around £55 and Eton pure Swiss non-iron cotton shirts are around £65. Designer labels such as Ralph Lauren will cost anything from £85.

There are two types of cuffs – single or double. Double cuffs allow you to wear cuff links, which can brighten up a plain suit. They should, however, be discreet and classy for work, made of gold or silver and not too big. Some shirts have a single cuff with both a button and a slit for links. This is not correct, though, so choose one or the other. Cuffs should be long enough to show at least a quarter of an inch below the sleeve of the jacket.

Short-sleeved shirts should not be worn with a business suit. If the weather is very warm, wear a light cotton shirt and roll up the sleeves when you take off your jacket.

Ties

You can inject your personality into an outfit with the tie you wear. Mary Spillane insists that a man should always choose his own ties, but what will he do with all the Christmas and birthday presents collected over the years? I agree that the choice must be personal, but sometimes a wife or partner will buy something that opens up new horizons, so keep an open mind.

Good-quality silk ties are best for the office. The heavier they are, the better they hold the knot. When buying, hold the tie by the narrow end to ensure it hangs straight. Handmade ties are still the best, and most come from Italy. To see whether yours is made by hand, look for a small piece of thread just inside the narrow end. If you pull it gently, the tie will start to bunch, proving it has not been sewn by a machine. Do not cut the thread off, otherwise the tie will fall to pieces!

Larger men look best in ties with bold patterns to match their build, while slighter men do not want to be swamped by loud designs. Handkerchiefs add colour to any suit or jacket, but although they should tone in with the tie, they should not match exactly, as this shows a lack of imagination. Treat ties with care. Try not to pull at the knot or crumple them away in a drawer and they will last for years.

Casual Wear

Men now spend much more money on casual clothes than they used to. Retailers have responded to the demand, and there is a good selection of casual wear for men to choose from. Designers such as Calvin Klein, Moschino and Joseph Abboud sell T-shirts from around £30 and sweatshirts from £80. Calvin Klein knitwear starts at £95. Joseph Abboud's will cost about £155 while a Versace sweater will be nearer £200. High-street shops are a good source of affordable casual wear. Try Next, Austin Reed, House of Fraser and Debenhams.

As styles in casual wear change each year, there is beginning to be a market in exchange clothes agencies for men. These agencies specialize in selling second-hand designer clothes.

Dinner Jackets

If you attend formal dinners or dances even a couple of times a year, it is worth investing in a dinner jacket. It will last for years, unless you grow out of it, and will not really date. Shirts can be frilly or plain to alter the look, and a cummerbund or waistcoat can also add a new dimension. Bow ties are usually bought already made up these days, but it is worth learning to tie a bow tie, as it is a sign of a gentleman!

Hats and Gloves

Hats are not worn as often as they used to be, but for special occasions they really make an outfit. You can buy hats at any department store from £25 upwards. Hatters such as Herbert Johnson or Gieves and Hawkes charge anything from £55 upwards for a Panama, trilby or fedora.

Underwear

Men tend to think that, as long as their nether garments are attractive and comfortable, there is nothing else to consider. However, a panty line on a man looks just as bad as it does on a woman, so for health and ease make sure underwear is not too tight! Ideally, choose underwear in natural fibres.

Socks are also best made of natural fibres such as silk, cotton or wool. They should be long enough not to show acres of hairy leg when you sit down, and always dark (black, charcoal, navy or grey) for business. Lightweight silk or cotton is nice for the summer and evening wear. To look classy, socks should be plain.

Summary

When choosing clothes:

- ■ Spend as much as you can on jackets, suits and a coat.
- ■ Make sure jackets do not pull or strain across the shoulders, or hang too loosely down the back.
- ■ Choose trousers that have a comfortable distance between crotch and waist, with hems that 'break' onto the shoe and are longer at the back.
- ■ Choose a good, firm fabric.
- ■ Mix and match clothes in colours that co-ordinate.
- ■ Check for hand stitching under the collar.
- ■ Opt for garments in natural fibres.
- ■ Make sure clothes are comfortable.

Caring for Clothes

Do not dry-clean clothes too often, as it is harmful to many fabrics. Clothes can sometimes smell a bit stale (after a night in a smoky atmosphere for example), and if you just want to freshen a garment, ask the cleaners to steam press it or hang it outside to get an airing, then sponge and press. Brush wool jackets regularly with a firm bristle brush to remove surface dirt. Always dry-clean suit jackets and trousers together (even the spare pairs), otherwise the colours will not match after a while.

Jackets are best stored on wooden hangers. Trousers should be pressed and then hung on good, firm hangers, as should shirts. Natural fabrics need a 'rest', so every so often leave them hanging outside the wardrobe for a day or two. The following tips are taken from a marvellous guide called 'Care Information' produced by Jaeger, which is available when purchasing their clothes.

Suede and Leather
Dry-clean garments regularly so that stains and dirt do not get ground in. This will also help maintain the even colour of the garment. Do not try to spot clean, otherwise you could leave a mark. Before wearing a suede or leather item, spray it first with Scotchguard or Weather Care. Brush suede jackets every so often with a special suede brush to remove surface dirt, then rub with a dry sponge to restore the pile. Should leather or suede get wet, leave it to dry before rubbing the surface with a dry cloth.

Corduroy
Trousers made from this hard-wearing cotton fabric should be dry-cleaned to keep their shape. Corduroy clothes should be ironed inside out on a low setting.

Silk
Silk should be dry-cleaned or hand-washed in luke-warm water using a mild detergent. I hate hand-washing, so I put any delicate garments on the cold rinse–short spin cycle of my machine, and I find it works very well. Colours, however, can run, so if the label says dry-clean, it means it! Do not leave silk to soak for long periods, and never wash silk ties, as they lose their shape. For best results, silk should be ironed while still damp on a medium setting (lower than cotton but higher than wool). Silk needs to breathe so do not store it in polythene bags. Keep it out of direct sunlight, as the colour will be affected. Aftershave lotions and deodorants will affect it too, so allow these to dry before dressing.

Linen
The creased look guarantees linen's authenticity. Some is washable and some is not (check the label). Jackets should be dry-cleaned, and linen is best ironed when damp.

Cotton
Most cotton garments can be machine-washed these days, but it is wise to examine the label first. Many shirts can be tumble-dried too, but again, it is advisable to check. Remove garments from the drier before they are completely dry, and press back into shape. Cotton is best ironed when

slightly damp or with a hot steam iron. If you do not have a steam iron, dampen the material with a cloth before ironing.

Knitwear

Good knitwear is usually made of wool or cotton and some is now machine-washable (check the label). Some sweaters have to be dry-cleaned, so check before buying. When machine-washing knitwear, the setting should never be too hot, nor the spin too long or fast, and items are best turned inside out to protect the fibres. Again, to wash anything delicate with 'hand-wash' on the label I use the cold rinse–short spin cycle with a mild liquid detergent, such as Dreft.

When you are hand-washing, make sure that the detergent has thoroughly dissolved in warm water before immersing the garment. Then gently squeeze and agitate it until clean before rinsing once in warm water and then in cold, four or five times until the water runs clear. Always dry wool (or any knitwear) away from direct heat, flat if possible. Cotton pullovers lose their shape easily, so they must be dried flat (on the bed placed on a couple of towels for example.)

If you are using a washing line, fold the garment over so that it will not lose its shape, and peg the sleeves of heavier jumpers. Do not tumble-dry knitwear or hang it over a radiator, as not only could the heat shrink garments, but it will also make the fibres brittle. Iron on a low setting inside out.

Stains

- Ink – splash with hot water immediately.
- Red wine – rub with salt or some white wine on a cloth and then wash down with tepid water.
- Grease – dab with eau de Cologne as soon as possible.
- Fruit or vegetable – wash the stain with water immediately, then rub well with Vanish soap before washing.

Shoes

Comfort is vital where shoes are concerned, as tired feet do nothing to improve performance or temper. Russell and Bromley have a good range of shoes in the £70–£170 range. Church's shoes are handmade and prices start around £165, while Trickers and Crockett and Jones cost between

£150–£200, the latter being made to order. Loake shoes are a very good buy, costing from £70, while Bally and Roland Cartier produce good shoes with a variety of styles from around £50. British designer Oliver Sweeney sells his shoes from £120; his trademark is an 'S' sewn into the side of the shoe. Shops like Cable and Co and Red or Dead sell up-to-the-minute fashion shoes starting at £40, and high-street stores like Dolcis stock a wide range of styles.

It is tempting to go for the latest trend, and that is fine as long as it does not break the bank. If you have a limited budget, however, the safest colours are black and brown. There is a great variety of smaller shops on the market now, some of whom make the shoes themselves, so if you find a cobbler that suits you, the investment is well worth it.

Once shoes bought at the lower end of the market start to wear, keep them for home use only. Expensive shoes wear more slowly and less noticeably. Always make sure the heels are not scuffed. To protect shoes from damp and dirt, always spray them with Scotchguard before wearing them for the first time, and repeat every time they get wet. Keep them clean, polish regularly and use a good shoe cream, such as Meltonin, to feed the leather. For patent leather, milk is a good polish, and you can also buy special sprays. Suede shoes should be brushed with a suede brush to remove any surface dirt. Most shoe shops stock shoe polishes, protectors and accessories.

Never dry wet shoes near heat. If you have splashed through a downpour, stuff the shoes with newspaper and let them dry naturally so that they keep their shape and colour. Use shoetrees, wooden if possible, and store shoes in boxes or on a rack, but not too close together.

The main points to remember are:

- Always buy leather uppers.
- Make sure shoes are comfortable.
- Protect them with a spray before wearing.
- Keep them clean.
- Store them with shoetrees.
- Get them reheeled and resoled as soon as they show signs of wear.

Briefcases

Marks and Spencer sell good quality, serviceable briefcases that cost around £70–£80. Briefcases will last for a reasonable length of time and still look good if you take care of them. Spray the case as soon as you buy it with Meltonian Scotchguard or Weather Care. You should also regularly clean the leather with a shoe cream – Meltonian and Punch produce creams in a range of colours for about £1.90 a jar. Never overfill briefcases, as this will put a strain on buckles and stitching. It is important to buy a new briefcase when your old one starts to look tatty.

The main points to remember are:

- Make sure buckles and handles are of good, strong design.
- Change it as soon as it begins to wear, unless it is very expensive.
- Keep it tidy inside as well as out!

EXERCISE

Although statistics tell us that, in the west, we eat less now than we did twenty years' ago, obesity is an increasing problem. The reason seems to be lack of exercise. An important part of presenting a positive image is being fit and energetic, whatever size we are, and a regular exercise routine is essential if we are to achieve this.

If, like me, the thought of jogging for miles appalls you and you cannot get near a gym, you can still build exercise into your daily routine. Try to cycle instead of using the car, for example, and take the stairs rather than the lift. If you have any damaged muscles or joints, walking and swimming are the best forms of exercise. Ensure you have proper cushioned shoes if you are going to do a lot of walking.

There are also exercises that you can do at home. Even ten minutes of exercise every other day is better than nothing. If you do not have a fitness plan or much time, try the routine outlined below. Put on your favourite music to help you exercise rhythmically. Choose music that has a steady beat, but is not too fast (I like the Rolling Stones, James Brown or any soul music). It is essential that you are comfortable with the speed of each exercise.

These exercises may be short and sweet, but I have devised them with the help of Sheena Storah, a Chartered Physiotherapist, who has a special interest in exercise and rehabilitation. She also kept Lancashire County Cricketers on their feet for over six years! These exercises do work on every part of your body and you can extend them as you wish. If you do nothing else, try and manage the stretching, as it will pay dividends.

1 Always start by gently warming up. March on the spot or step on and off the bottom stair or a shallow step for about four minutes. Next comes the stretch. Try to touch the ceiling! Reach up as high as you can until you feel your spine lengthen, being careful not to push your head back too far, as this can strain the neck. Do this to the count of twenty.

2 Stand with your legs apart, put your hands on your hips and, keeping your back straight, bend your knees, keeping them in line with the toes. Repeat twenty times.

3 Keeping your hands on your hips and your back straight, gently swing the body from side to side, twenty times.

4 Put your hands in the air and stretch up, then drop your arms towards your toes. Lower your head and shoulders towards the floor with knees slightly bent. Try this ten times.

5 Place fingertips together level with your chest and push out your arms twenty times. Next, spread the arms out and back horizontally another twenty times.

6 Stretch your arms out in front of you, cross them at the wrist with palms facing, and then clasp hands together. Raise both arms above your head and stretch up as far as you can. Now 'pulse' them twenty times.

7 Lie flat on the floor and bring each knee up to your chin in turn, twenty times.

8 Stay on the floor with your knees bent. Flatten the hollow of your back into the floor, pulling your tummy in tight. Gently lift your head and shoulders a little, twenty times.

9 Stand up slowly. With both hands, hold on to a sturdy piece of furniture (the dining-room table or a chest of drawers), arms outstretched. Raise one leg behind you, then the other. Repeat twenty times.

10 Run on the spot for as long as you can before it feels uncomfortable.

There are also all kinds of fitness tapes and videos available, so try and find one that works for you. Jane Fonda has produced several, as has Callan Pinkney, the founder of Callanetics, and Mr Motivator, to name just a few.

Although many of these products are aimed at men and women, videos and tapes are now available marketed just for men.

Keeping fit really is essential as far as prolonging life is concerned. If you are at all worried about starting an exercise regime, go and see your doctor first. If you keep fit you feel well, and if you feel well, you look good!

DIET

To look good, feel good and create a positive image, we need to eat foods that replenish cells quickly, provide energy and give us pleasure too. Skin, nails and hair suffer if our diet is not well balanced, and low energy levels can affect confidence in both professional and personal life.

These days, there is more pressure on men to be slim than there used to be. For many, however, it is not what nature intended, so look at your body realistically and ask yourself how easy it is going to be to achieve the shape and weight you want. Although it is important not to fight too hard against nature, a good diet and regular exercise are essential elements of a healthy lifestyle. A diet high in fat, sugar and processed foods and low in fibre is clearly hazardous to health. If you are a 'picker' you can consume a large amount of food without even realizing it. As a test, write down every mouthful of food that you eat during the course of one day; you may well be horrified by how much it can amount to. If you are an enthusiastic cook who tastes the food as you go along, try an experiment. For every spoonful you taste, put one in a bowl. Some people find they have eaten a meal before they have even finished cooking! Moderation in all things is the key to stress-free dieting.

If I want to lose a few pounds, I cut out all junk and fatty foods, drink plenty of water and eat smaller portions, making sure I chew the food properly. It really can be as simple as that. Cutting down on fat and eating fruit instead of crisps or snack bars will also help. It is a good idea to have two or three alcohol-free days a week. Drinking water helps clear the system of toxins, and moreover fills a hunger gap between meals; a couple of glasses drunk just before a meal will help you eat less. Our thirst 'pangs', which decrease as we get older, are often mistaken for hunger pangs. If you are feeling tired or develop a mild headache, it can be a sign of dehydration, and a glass of water will often put you right. A litre a day is the minimum everyone should drink, and it is better uncarbonated. If you do not find the thought of plain water particularly palatable, try adding a few slices of lemon, orange or mint to a jug of water and leaving it in the fridge over night.

Key points for a healthy diet and well-tuned body:

- Drink at least a litre of water a day.
- Eat as much fresh food as you can.
- Cut out junk food and sugary or fizzy drinks.
- Choose fish rather than too much red meat.
- Limit your intake of fat.
- Keep tea, coffee and alcohol consumption to a minimum.
- Eat dairy products sparingly.
- Make sure you eat a balanced diet of protein, carbohydrate and fresh, raw fruit and vegetables every day (eat as many raw vegetables as you can, but do not eat too much fruit – our ancestors only ate it in season, and too much acid can cause spots).
- Remember – most things are all right in moderation!

Detox Your System

If you want to give your system a pick-me-up and lose a couple of pounds into the bargain, you might like to try an occasional 'detoxing' day, during which you eat only fruit and drink as much water as you can. As an alternative to fruit, brown rice mixed with raw or cooked vegetables is a good purifier too. Choose a day when you are unlikely to be running a hectic schedule or under too much stress.

Vitamins and Mineral Supplements

I take vitamin and mineral supplements in the winter, or if I am working particularly hard. I believe they keep me fairly free of colds, as well as improving my skin, nails and hair. Do not expect instant benefits, however, as it takes two or three months to notice the difference. Your local health-food shop can give you advice on which supplements are right for you. Some supplements can be dangerous if taken in too high a dosage, so always read the instructions carefully, and consult your doctor if you have any doubts. For further information on nutritional supplements, see *Thorsons Complete Guide to Vitamins and Minerals* (Thorsons, 1989).

COMPLEMENTARY THERAPIES

There is a growing interest in complementary therapies, so called because they are intended to be used alongside conventional medicine, although for many ailments they can provide an effective treatment on their own. Complementary therapies are perceived as more gentle than conventional medicine as they tend not to be associated with as many side-effects, and some therapies, such as massage and aromatherapy, are very pleasant to receive.

Homoeopathy

Homoeopathy is based on the principle 'like cures like'. A homoeopathic remedy that produces particular symptoms in a healthy person will be used to cure the same symptoms in an ill person. Although homoeopathy can be a good alternative to prescribed drugs, you should always consult your doctor first if you feel you have a problem.

To find a qualified homoeopath in your area, contact the British Homoeopathic Association, 27a Devonshire Street, London W1N 1RJ or the Society of Homoeopaths, 2 Artizan Road, Northampton NN1 4HU. If you want to find out more about homoeopathy, there are now many books available, and the main commercial suppliers of homoeopathic remedies, Nelsons and Weleda, produce easy-to-read booklets which are available from health-food shops and many pharmacies. Here are just a few of the myriad remedies on offer (the normal dosage is two tablets taken every hour for six doses, then three times daily until better):

- Aconite 6 – treats colds and flu; also has a calming influence, so is useful to take before an interview, for example.
- Arnica 6 – marvellous rubbed on bruises or strains; can be taken orally if you are mentally or physically tired.
- Arsen. Alb. 6 – helps cure food poisoning, vomiting and a very runny cold. It is important to remember that sickness and diarrhoea are nature's way of cleansing the system, but if symptoms persist, see your doctor.
- Gelsemium 6 – useful for flu and real apprehension, such as exam nerves.
- Hamemmelis – very good for keeping varicose veins at bay.
- Nux vomica – an indigestion remedy. It helps with hangovers too!

■ Rhus. tox. 6 – very good for rheumatic pain and strain after long day on the golf course or a lot of physical exercise.

Herbal Remedies

Herbalism is the use of plants to treat ailments. Herbal remedies come in a variety of forms – capsules, tinctures, infusions, decoctions, ointments and compresses. Consult a herbalist before taking any specific remedies.
Contact the General Council and Register of Consultant Herbalists, Grosvenor House, 40 Sea Way, Middleton-on-Sea, West Sussex PO22 7SA or the National Institute of Medical Herbalists, 9 Palace Gate, Exeter EX1 1JA.
Here are some herbal remedies obtainable in capsule form from chemists and health-food shops:

■ Garlic – often called 'nature's antibiotic', it is marvellous for cleansing the blood and enhances immune responses. It is usually deodorized.

■ Ethinacea – very good for colds and flu as it has antiviral and antibacterial properties.

■ Eyebright – relieves discomfort of eyestrain or minor eye irritations and hay fever.

■ Hawthorn berry – acts as a tonic for the heart.

■ Korean ginseng – known as 'the queen of herbs', it is probably the oldest and most widely used herb in the world. Slowly builds energy and stamina over a period of weeks.

■ Barley tablets – an excellent source of vitamins, proteins and minerals.

■ Feverfew – alleviates migraines and headaches.

■ Red raspberry leaves – a tonic for the prostate gland.

■ Ginger – used in the east for over 2000 years, it helps stimulate the circulation and relaxes blood vessels.

■ Liquorice root – aids digestion, as it limits the production of acid in the system.

■ Yucca – helps alleviate the problems of arthritis, rheumatism and gout.

■ Kelp – rich in calcium, potassium and magnesium; wonderful for hair and nails.

■ Dandelion root – a diuretic and a good tonic for the liver.

■ Red clover – good for chronic skin problems such as eczema and psoriasis.

■ Royal jelly – a good source of energy.

Herbal teas are a marvellous alternative to drinking lots of coffee or traditional tea as they are caffeine-free and have beneficial properties:

- Camomile – helps you relax and aids digestion. Best drunk at bedtime.
- Peppermint – helps inject a bit of 'pep', as the name implies. Also aids digestion.
- Lemon – highly refreshing and contains vitamin C.
- Nettle – helps relieve the symptoms of hay fever.

A wide variety of fruit teas is also available. These are also caffeine-free.

Massage

Massage is a wonderful way in which to relax. If you are frantically busy, try to find time for a regular massage (possibly during your lunch hour), as the amount of energy that can be restored by a period of deep relaxation is enormous. A massage will not only help relax tense muscles and calm frayed nerves, it will also stimulate the blood supply and help release toxins that build up in the muscles. After a massage, drink plenty of water to enable your system to flush out as much waste as possible. As with all therapists, choose a massage practitioner whose certificate of competence is prominently displayed.

Reflexology

Reflexology is a stimulating and revitalizing experience, and can be of real benefit, especially in times of stress. This therapy is based on the theory that energy channels, known as zones or meridians, pass through every organ of the body and end in the feet, which contain 72,000 nerve endings. The Chinese have used this treatment for thousands of years and it is becoming increasingly popular in the west. By massaging specific areas of the feet, reflexologists are able to work on corresponding areas of the body. It can prove beneficial for many complaints, such as backache, migraine, acne, eczema and psoriasis. I visited a reflexologist when I was suffering from a slight kidney infection. When the reflexologist came to massage that particular point of the foot, it was uncomfortable. She advised me to see my doctor to be on the safe side, but after the massage I felt a lot better.

SKIN CARE

We all aim for healthy, glowing skin. Diet plays a very important part in skin care (*see 'Diet', pages 16 – 17 for more information*), and deep sleep is essential for the body to renew itself. While we are asleep, our cells divide at a much faster rate and a growth hormone is released into the bloodstream causing regeneration. Some people can function on four or five hours' sleep a night, while others need nine or ten. Whether you need little or lots of sleep, always listen to your body when it tells you it is tired.

More and more men are using skin-care products these days, and there are some new and exciting products on offer. If you are unsure about the benefits of using a moisturizer and toner, never mind a 'Scruffing Lotion', the male teams in the men's departments of larger stores will be only too pleased to help and advise. Clinique has a comprehensive range to suit all skin types. After a computerized analysis telling you what your skin needs, the Clinique technicians work out a skin-care routine for you. There is facial soap, a 'Scruffing Lotion' that removes particles of dead skin and 'M Lotion' that acts as a moisturizer. 'Face Lotion Oil Free Formula' moisturizes oily skin without leaving that greasy feeling so many men dislike, and it is also useful in hot climates. Prices start from £9.99 to about £17, and a little of these products go a long way. The Lab Series from Aramis contains 'Skin Clearing Solution' from £12.99, 'Instant Moisture Complex' at around £19.99 and 'Lift Off Alpha-Hydroxy Moisture Complex' which is fragrance-free and has an everyday sun screen of SPF 7.

Facial scrubs that remove any excess grease, dirt and dead skin cells are available from the Body Shop, as are a range of cleansers, moisturizing and toning lotions suitable for men and women, starting at around £4.99. Boots and Marks and Spencer also do a useful range of skin-care products in the £5–£15 bracket.

A dermatologist friend of mine once told me that a wipe with a damp sponge is all skin needs to keep it clean. While this may be the case for people who do not travel on tube trains or live in polluted cities, most of us need to work a little harder on our skin-care routine. Pollution levels are so much higher than they used to be that the skin is subjected to far more harmful chemicals these days, and the thinning of the ozone layer also has a significant effect. Protecting and cleansing are the order of the day. Hands too, should be kept well moisturized. It is advisable to wear a moisturizer with UVA and UVB screens all the year round, as it will help guard against everyday contamination as well as harmful rays. Brand names to look out for include Ambre Solaire and E45. Clinique make a 'Non-Streak Bronzer' for men, which gives colour as well as moisture and protection. Auto-bronzers are becoming increasingly popular with businessmen in the summer. Prices range from £5.99–£17. E45 is very good as an inexpensive night cream to soften skin that has been exposed to sun or wind, especially after a day on the golf course, or after any outdoor sport such as windsurfing, sailing, fishing, skiing, riding or rugby.

Facial washes, cleansing bars and liquid gels (which are more gentle than the former) are effective in making sure the skin on the face is really clean without having the drying effects associated with most hand soaps. Any spots or blemishes can be hidden with a concealer such as 'Touche Eclat' by Yves Saint Laurent, which costs around £17 but lasts for ages.

Having a facial is not only good for the skin, as it aids circulation, but it is also a marvellously relaxing experience. If it was enjoyed by everyone at least once a month, I am sure it could replace valium as a stress reliever. The same goes for massage of any kind. Massage treatments using aromatherapy oils are very popular, but make sure you wear easily washable clothes after you have one, as the oils can stain clothes, especially silk.

If you are troubled with spots, use a fresh piece of cotton wool to clean each affected area, and dab carefully with cleanser in order not to spread the infection. You can buy cleansing products that have been specially formulated to fight spots, such as Oxy 5 or 10 and Biactol. If you have sensitive skin, however, you should test such products before using them in case you have a reaction. Apply some to a small area of the lower part of your face and leave overnight.

To summarize the main points of skin care for men:

- Eat a well-balanced diet.
- Clean the face well at night and again in the morning.
- Use a daytime moisturizer with a built-in sunscreen.
- If in doubt about which products you should use, have a skin-care analysis.

HAIR

Your hair should be your crowning glory, but a poor diet, smoking, medication and too many late nights can all contribute to poor hair condition. A good diet is fundamental (*see 'Diet', pages 16 – 17*), as is a good haircut that shows your face to best advantage. This will cost you anything from £5 to £25 depending on the stylist and salon, and will last six to eight weeks before it starts to look out of shape.

Finding a Stylist

Choosing a hairdresser is as much down to personal chemistry as anything else – provided that he or she is competent. The image of the staff and the appearance of the clients will help you get an idea of the sort of stylists that work there. If, for example, the clothes are extreme, the cuts are likely to be adventurous too. I went into a new hair salon recently and was slightly confused when asked if I wanted 'an artistic director'. When I looked blank, the receptionist asked if I wanted a 'senior stylist'. That was exactly what I wanted – preferably without the delusions of grandeur!

The busiest stylists are not always the best. A newly qualified hairdresser can be just as good, so ask around and look at your friends, especially the ones who have similar hair and colouring. A satisfied customer can only be a good advertisement. When you have found a stylist you trust, who listens to what you want and cuts your hair in a style that suits you, stay with him or her!

Choosing a Style

If you have a good idea of the style you want, try and find a picture to take with you to the salon. Alternatively, if you have no idea, ask to look through some magazines when you arrive for inspiration. It is important, however, to listen to the advice of your stylist. If the style you long for will not suit you, he or she will explain this to you and suggest something more appropriate. Give your stylist a chance to get to know you and your hair. Any reasonable salon is happy to reappraise a cut if you do not like it, but you cannot expect them to be so willing if you have flatly gone against their advice.

Shampoo and Conditioner

Keeping hair in good condition also requires a good shampoo, especially if you wash it every day. Most shampoos are detergent-based, which means they are alkaline and cheaper to make, but harsher for the hair. 'Two-in-one' shampoo and conditioners are useful if you are in a hurry, but they do not really nourish the hair. They are also alkaline, and the gloss they give comes from silicone in the conditioner. Most hairdressers do not recommend them.

Shampoos like Nutra-clenz 'Nucleic A' or those produced by KMS, Paul Mitchell and Redken are acid-based, which matches the natural pH-balance of the hair. They are more expensive but it is worth paying extra, and that goes for conditioners too. Do not expect instant results, however, as it will take a month or six weeks to see the real benefits.

There are several anti-dandruff shampoos on the market, including Clinique's 'Special Help Shampoo'. Other brands to look out for are KMS and the Svenson Hair Clinic, which specializes in scalp problems. Baby shampoo is very pure, and is good to use for a time if the scalp is very sensitive. Paul Mitchell products include a versatile range of preparations and shampoos. Their 'Clean Scalp Shampoo' is ideal for everyday use.

Hair Care

Brushing helps the scalp as it removes any dry skin, and massaging the scalp encourages hair growth. Hairbrushes and combs should be cleaned regularly. To avoid splitting the hair, always use a brush which has bristles with rounded ends.

Hair obviously needs to be kept clean, but too much washing and brushing can stimulate the glands, making them produce more oil. An egg cup of lemon juice dissolved in a jug of water will help remove excess oil from the hair, and an egg cup of cider vinegar in rinsing water can help restore the pH-balance if you have been using alkaline-based shampoos and 'leave-in' conditioners for a long time.

Hair Styling

Do not use a very hot dryer on your hair, as this can be damaging. It is best to leave hair to dry for a while before blowing it, as it gives it more body. Mousse will also help to give extra lift, and there are a number of hairsprays for men in the shops now. Clinique make two: 'Hair Programme Lotion' and 'Non-Fragranced Hairspray'.

Coloured Hair

Coloured hair must be retouched at the roots as soon as regrowth appears. Hair-colouring technology has advanced dramatically over the last few years. Ask your hairdresser which is the right preparation for you. There are hundreds of home hair-colouring kits on the market. These range from the shampoo-in variety that wash out after a few weeks, such as 'Harmony', to the more permanent types made by companies like Wella and Schwarzkopf. You can buy them from as little as £4.99.

Keep these points in mind if you want your crowning glory to be just that:

- Find a good hairdresser!
- Eat a well-balanced diet.
- Choose a hairstyle that suits your type of hair.
- Get a good haircut.
- Use an acid-based shampoo and conditioner.

Beards, Moustaches and Eyebrows

Beards and moustaches should be kept trimmed, and any unwanted hair (in ears or nostrils) should be carefully seen to with a pair of nail scissors. Eyebrows that meet in the middle are best plucked, as they give an impression of shiftiness, and very thick brows could also do with tidying up. If you do not want to do this yourself, a barber or hairdresser should do it for you.

GLASSES

The wrong shape of glasses can spoil the handsomest of faces. However much you may like a particular style, do make sure it suits you before you buy what can be an expensive item. The top of the spectacles should be in line with your eyebrows, and the bottom should be no lower than the top of your cheekbones. If in doubt, ask your optician for advice.

Eyes should be checked regularly, as they are an early-warning system for a number of ailments, including glaucoma and high blood pressure. If you wear contact lenses, make sure you keep them really clean or they can cause permanent damage to the eyes.

TEETH

It is very difficult to have a sparkling smile if your teeth are crooked or dingy. The world of cosmetic dentistry has produced marvels over the last few years, but with more and more dentists going into private practice, the cost of getting your teeth done is growing. There are several insurance plans available, which may be worth your investment if you think you may need work in the future. If your teeth do not fit your mouth properly it is impossible to speak clearly, but it is never too late to visit an orthodontist. Caps, crowns, bridges and veneers can transform your face, never mind your mouth.

It is wise to have a check-up at least twice a year, and to visit the hygienist every few months for a clean and polish. Cleaning teeth regularly is part of everybody's routine, but it is important to use dental floss and a good brush. Tea, coffee, red wine and tobacco can stain the teeth, so use a stain-removing toothpaste or a tooth-whitener such as 'Pearl Drops' every now and then.

NAILS

If I want to feel really good I go and have a manicure. Men often fail to realize how much their nails are noticed. They must always be clean, and if they are not looking too tidy, a manicure is a relaxing, as well as an aesthetic, treatment.

Tips for nail care:

- Keep nails spotlessly clean.
- Keep them short.
- Manicure regularly.

2

---

first impressions

Whether we like it or not, the way we dress influences the way in which we are perceived and received by others. Police descriptions of suspects always mention their clothes, size and colouring, as these are the first things we notice. First impressions are powerful. If our first impression of someone is negative, it will stay with us for a long time, making it very difficult to replace it with a positive image. And it is not just our appearance that creates the first impression – analysts claim that our reaction to others is judged thus:

- 58 per cent on how we look.
- 35 per cent on how we sound.
- 7 per cent on what we say.

You have to decide what image you want to impress upon people, and try to make sure you achieve it. This can, however, be difficult. If, for example, you are at the beginning of your career, you might not yet be sure of the image you want to portray.

First impressions can have a significant effect on various aspects of your life, some more serious than others. As far as the law is concerned, the trial of O. J. Simpson provided an interesting example. It was at that time that

American lawyers started doing 'make-overs' on witnesses so that they promoted a positive image and were more acceptable to juries. Whether this was right or wrong, it shows the power and importance of the image you project and the impression you leave.

We make immediate judgements about whom we want to talk to based on appearance and body language. This is followed by how people sound, not by what they are saying. Whether someone is small or tall, fat or skinny all has a bearing on how we react to that person. You have to be aware of how your basic physique comes across and compensate for it if necessary.

What about beards and moustaches? To some people, a beard immediately starts a train of thought that asks 'why does this man want to be different from other people?'. Men grow beards and moustaches for a variety of reasons. It may be to compensate for lack of hair on the head; it may be because they hate shaving; or it may be because they *do* want to stand out from the crowd. But whatever the reason, they should be aware of the image they are projecting and how it might be interpreted or misinterpreted.

When people say 'Oh, you're not what I expected at all!', ask them why, and find out how they did picture you. It is a good thing to stand back and let other people tell you how they see you, as we all have a set idea of the image we portray to the world, but it might not be the one we think it is.

THE VISUAL IMAGE

The visual image is very important as it is the first impression people have of you before you open your mouth. Communication comes from the face and the eyes, and a person's attractiveness is down to their expression, not the way their features are arranged. Comedian Ken Dodd says that the shortest distance between two people is a smile! A smiling face is an appealing face, giving an agreeable first impression. A really bright smile can have an amazing effect. It can light up a plain face and, more importantly, break down the invisible barriers that exist between us all.

Our expressions can have a material effect on the way we think and the way we feel. Some psychologists claim that different expressions affect the flow of blood to the brain, causing positive or negative feelings. Negative feelings can show on our faces in later years. Think positive and you will look positive. Laughter and smiling are said to increase the flow, producing positive emotions. It is worth a try anyway!

For a smile to create a positive impression, it must be genuine. There are several types of smile:

■ A genuine smile is shown by both corners of the mouth turning up. Sometimes the teeth are shown and sometimes not.

■ The miserable smile is hiding distress or unhappiness, usually as a front before others. It is characterized by a lack of symmetry, with one side seeming not to smile at all.

■ The false smile signals insincerity. It usually lasts longer than a real one and does not reach the eyes, which remain cold or hard.

A good, strong smile is a winning asset, so do not be afraid to use it! Laughter, too, is strong medicine, helping us to achieve a natural high and a release from tension, which is why some people (especially children) laugh when they are in trouble. It is said that one minute of laughter can provide up to forty-five minutes of relaxation, enabling the body to unwind. Happy people not only appear more relaxed – they usually are.

Your clothes and general appearance will also create a strong first impression. People will instantly decide whether you are a tidy or untidy person, imaginative or stylish. Men are fortunate when it comes to first impressions as they get more of a chance to speak their way into a situation, whereas first impressions of women tend to be formed by their appearance alone.

Image Consultants

If you are unsure of the impression you are making, there are firms of image consultants all over the country who will check the colours that suit you and give useful advice. 'Color Me Beautiful' (CMB) has a list of consultants available throughout the UK as does 'First Impressions'. (For the addresses of these organizations, *see Chapter 1*.) Image consultants will take your occupation and lifestyle into consideration, and advise you on how to dress appropriately. Although you want to look to create a positive impression, it is important that what you wear does not distract others from what you do. For example, a doctor dressed in jeans and a T-shirt, rather than a crisp white coat, might have difficulty in gaining the trust of his patients.

A surveyor working on a building site dressed in a city suit would raise the same doubts in contractors' minds.

Ethnic Issues

Sadly, racism does exist, and when you apply for a job it is a potential issue which unfortunately cannot be ignored. The colour of someone's skin obviously makes an impression. A white person applying for a job cooking in a Chinese restaurant would have more difficulty convincing the owner that he was right for the post than someone from Hong Kong. Whatever the colour of your skin, it is essential to put forward your positive points, be realistic about the role you are pursuing and believe in yourself. If you are right for the position and that firm does not employ you, then they are the ones who are losing out.

The actor Lenny Henry believes in the importance of a strong self-image. 'If you think you are rubbish and go out expecting the worst, then it will happen.' First impressions, too, are vital. When he is carrying out auditions, he makes up his mind about someone within the first two minutes. 'Never limit yourself in your search for a job,' he advises. 'Make some effort to look the part. If you go in wearing a ripped silk parachute suit, nobody will take you seriously. Smile when you meet people, get to business when you sit down and don't lose your sense of humour.' Be prepared and be positive is his advice. He also thinks that 'what goes around, comes around', and finds that people respond to kindness, particularly in stressful situations, such as an interview or audition. A positive impression for Lenny means projecting your personality and showing you have the ability to work hard and fit in.

Style

Although men's fashion changes much more slowly than women's, it is important to move with the times and wear clothes that are up to date (especially trousers, shirts and ties). Creases, tears, holes, stains, frayed collars and loose buttons all go towards making a negative first impression.

Earlier I touched on what makes 'style', but how do you achieve it? The first thing is to keep your clothes in excellent condition. They must always be clean – a line of grime round a collar will ruin an otherwise stylish ensemble. Being stylish takes time and effort. You need to check your clothes regularly to ensure they are in tip-top condition whenever you need them.

Find out what colours suit you. If you do not want to go to image consultants, ask friends, family, shop assistants and colleagues. When you have decided on your colour range, buy clothes that will mix and match. Take, for example, a pair of trousers. Why not look for a colour and style that will go with a particular:

- jacket
- jersey
- T-shirt
- shirt?

Add different belts and shoes, and you now have four different 'looks'. Do the same with jerseys, jeans, shirts and jackets. You might think that choosing something like a T-shirt is simple; but to give the outfit 'style' there needs to be a theme, whether it is the cut, the pattern or the colour. However super a particular item of clothing may be, if you have nothing to wear it with, it is a waste of money because it will never look right.

But what about the cut that will make the most of your particular build? The only way to find out what flatters you most is to try things on. Bear in mind that your body shape is likely to change with age, so the clothes that suited you ten years' ago may be unflattering now. It is a good idea to put on things that you cannot afford as well as those you can. It may be rather frustrating, but it will help you gain a concept of quality and cut, and give you something to save up for!

Dressing smartly when you are shopping for clothes means you will be treated with more respect by shop assistants and therefore get much better service. You should also wear the type of shoes that will go with the outfit you intend to buy – trainers never did much for a pinstripe suit – otherwise you will not see the whole picture. While assistants are there to sell the clothes, if you tell them that you are trying to establish a particular style, they are usually helpful and should give reasonably unbiased advice.

Age and personality have a lot to do with style. However much you may want to wear trendy, up-to-the-minute fashion that will get you noticed, you will never look 'stylish' if you feel uncomfortable. You have to be able to wear your clothes with pride and confidence. The most stunning outfit worn by somebody with drooping shoulders and a hanging head will look nothing, whereas a suit from Marks and Spencer worn with confidence can look a million dollars. You can put your own touches to any outfit by adding:

- an individual tie or cravat
- a silk handkerchief
- attractive cufflinks
- an unusual belt or pair of braces
- a handmade shirt
- distinctive boots or shoes
- a good watch.

To make the right impression and create a positive image, clothes should be worn like a second skin, reflecting your mood and character. If you go out of the door first thing in the morning knowing you are wearing the wrong thing, it can affect your performance all day; so go back in and change! But whether you are going out to paint the town or merely to meet friends at the pub, your clothes must be clean, pressed, co-ordinated and distinctive to create that certain something called 'style'.

Clothes Shopping

While I cannot give individual advice as to where you might shop for your clothes, here are some guidelines. I have not included designer clothes in this section.

18–25 Age Range

You can get away with much more when you are young, so shop around and mix some expensive items with cheaper ones. Try:

- Debenhams
- Next
- Burtons
- Armani

25–45 Age Range

You are probably spending a little more on specific outfits as you progress up the ladder. Quality rather than quantity should be the order of the day. Try:

- Principles for Men
- Marks and Spencer
- Jaeger Man
- Armani

45-plus Age Range
You are probably still shopping at many of the above if you are in your forties or fifties, but here are a few more suggestions:

- Gieves and Hawkes
- Austin Reed
- Bernard Wetherill

Style on a Budget
We all need to know how to make the right impression without breaking the bank, so here are a few tips for a very basic capsule wardrobe for work:

- a suit (single-breasted and navy if you are not going to buy a blazer)
- a well-cut blazer or jacket
- two pairs of trousers – one grey or stone
- a pair of jeans (for weekend courses and training days)
- five shirts in a range of pastel colours (at least two should be white)
- ties and handkerchiefs to complement (but not match) the shirts
- a briefcase
- one pair of braces
- black shoes
- a warm coat or mac.

Your working wardrobe obviously depends on what line of work you are in, but this is the absolute minimum you can get away with to look professional for most jobs, and it will cost you anything from £900. If you can plan ahead, buy in the sales in order to pick up some bargains and really save money.

Body Language
How we behave is as important as what we wear. The way we enter a room, the way we stand and sit and the way we speak all help to create that first impression. Chapter 3 looks at improving body language and vocal

technique, but for now we will concentrate on the positive and negative conclusions that can be drawn from how we conduct ourselves.

Nerves

There are several clues that tell us when someone is nervous. A dry mouth, licking of the lips, throat clearing, foot tapping, scratching and rapid breathing are obvious signs, and they can give a very negative impression. I will be giving some tips on controlling nerves in Chapters 5 and 6.

Touch

Our skin is a massive sensory organ sending messages to the brain. Touch is very important to most animals, especially humans. We all feel better when we have had some sun on our backs, and a massage leaves the body feeling both stimulated and relaxed. Tactile people are often more popular than those who never touch, as it enables us, both consciously and subconsciously, to get closer to each other.

We have to be careful not to invade someone's personal space, but a brief squeeze of the hand or a touch on the arm can do much to reassure, comfort or cajole.

Stance

When you walk into a room, stand tall with your head up and your gaze directed at the person to whom you are going to talk. This automatically makes you look and feel confident and at ease. It does not mean putting your nose in the air (which gives the impression of haughtiness), but standing with your shoulders back and your head facing forward. If you have initiated the meeting, walk towards the other person and offer your hand.

The Handshake

A firm handshake is vital. I certainly find it makes a strong impression on me. If someone in a powerful position offers me a 'limp lettuce' or a 'wet fish', I always question how they got where they did, and wonder where their weak point is. Some men (and women) today tend to go overboard and are almost fierce in the way they grasp your unsuspecting paw. There is no need to overdo it! It is quite sufficient to take the hand, clasp it firmly and then let go. It can be interesting to watch out for personality traits in the way a hand is proffered:

- The person to offer the hand first is generally the most assertive.
- The strength of contact can be an indicator of character.
- If no hand is offered in return, that person is either very shy, has a hygiene phobia or is trying to put you down!
- A dominant handshake is offered with the palm face down.
- A submissive handshake is when the palm faces up.
- Aim for equal status – arm outstretched with the hand horizontal, thumb facing upwards.

Posture

There is a big difference between confidence and arrogance. Overconfidence or superiority is often displayed by the way someone sits. This could be with the hands clasped behind the head, or leaning back in the chair with legs outstretched and ankles crossed. A prospective employer or future client adopting this position could well be playing for effect to see how you react to such rudeness. Someone who is sitting forward in the chair or leaning on a desk, perhaps forming a 'steeple' with the fingers, is much more likely to be listening with interest to what you have to say. Glasses often have a role to play. Some people gain thinking time by polishing their glasses or slowly and deliberately folding them before asking the next question.

To create a positive impression you should aim to:

- Look alert.
- Sit straight (without looking as though you have a poker down your back).
- Keep your head up, with your eye line directed at the person in front of you.
- Keep hands clasped loosely unless you are taking notes.

Obviously, the more familiar you are with the people and the circumstances, the more your posture will relax.

Eye Contact

Eye contact is critical. You cannot read another person's character unless you can see into his or her eyes. Our pupils unconsciously dilate when we find somebody attractive, and we look into their eyes for longer. But watch out for shifts in eye contact; it could mean that you are starting to talk too much. Aim for a direct gaze but not an unblinking stare. When we are speaking to someone we automatically look first into one eye, then the other, down to the mouth and back to the eyes again, so you can consciously alter your eye line if you are becoming uncomfortable.

Where to Sit

Where you sit, especially in a sales or interview situation, can make quite an impression. For a friendly meeting or chat, the best position is to sit diagonally across a table. If you want to encourage trust, sit next to someone as it is less confrontational. If you want to negotiate a deal, it is best not to sit opposite your potential customer as this can encourage competitive feelings; again, a diagonal position is best.

Reading Body Language

I am sure you have been to parties where you knew instantly that you were not going to enjoy the evening. And you have probably been to interviews where, the minute you walked into the reception, you knew you would not fit in to that company.

The impression a person, a place or an organization makes on you is very important. Try to beware of jumping to instant conclusions, however, especially about people. Some of us are better at evaluating our fellows than others, and although we should take notice of initial reactions, they must not prejudice us against exploring further. This is particularly the case if you are taking part in the selection process for jobs. A candidate for a teaching post, for example, may not initially give the impression that he or she could control a class of unruly adolescents. Further investigation, however, may confirm that the candidate has proved more than a match for the situation in the past and is exactly right for the job.

How do you spot someone who is insincere or lying? Simple things like a shifty gaze and fidgety gestures should put you on your guard. So should a lot of face touching or pulling of the ear lobes. This habit usually stems from childhood – children will cover their mouths when lying, almost as if they want to stop the words coming out. Reading body language has to be done with great caution, however, and the particular circumstances taken into account. An untruthful person often crosses both the arms and legs simultaneously when telling a lie, but so does someone who is in a hurry and wants the conversation to close, or very tired and is trying to inject some adrenaline into their system.

When we talk, most of us use our hands to emphasize points, and the way in which we use them can be very revealing. When someone is lying they tend to clasp the hands together or push them deep into their pockets in case their hands give them away. An indication that the hands are disagreeing with the mouth is evident when the palms face upwards in what is known as the 'hand-shrug'. If somebody is unsure of their facts they will often use this gesture.

Positive Gestures
You cannot manufacture positive body language. If you try to do so, it will have the opposite effect, giving an impression of insincerity. There are, however, positive signs to look out for in others:

- Hand resting on the cheek – means evaluation or analysis.
- Hand stroking chin – signals consideration.
- Steepling the fingers – displays confidence.
- Rubbing hands together quickly – anticipation!
- Hands pressed together – persuasion.
- Leaning forward – denotes active listening.
- Direct eye contact – indicates honesty and interest.
- Eyebrow lift – this quick movement says someone is glad to see you.
- Head held up – marks confidence and integrity.
- A smile – the genuine article shows a sincere greeting.

Personal chemistry matters enormously in your dealings with people – on a professional and a social level – so try to listen to what other people have to say and put yourself in their position before you make up too much of your mind about them. Consider the whole case; do not just go on the first impression.

Gestures to Avoid
Body language must be sincere in order to create the right impression. It is vital that the mind and body are in agreement when we speak, as anyone who has read even a little on the subject will see something that will give us away! Avoid the following negative gestures:

■   Fidgeting with the hands.

■   Rubbing the nose or eyes.

■   Rubbing the hands slowly together (this often denotes lying or insincerity).

■   Excessive stroking of the cheek or chin.

■   Slouching in the chair.

■   Crossing arms over the chest (forming the 'barrier' position).

■   Clenched fists.

■   Pointing with the finger to emphasize points.

■   Shifty eye contact.

■   Looking out of the window or at the ceiling.

■   A blank expression.

■   Foot tapping.

■   Moving the ankles from side to side.

■   Too much crossing of arms and legs.

Sexual Signals

Much of our positive body language happens unconsciously, and the way we react to people shows itself in different ways. Next time you are at a party or meeting, see if you can spot the signs. A man will often begin to smarten himself up at the approach of an attractive woman – a bit like a male bird fluffing out its feathers. Adjusting clothes, straightening the tie and smoothing the hair are all signs of interest, and help make what he hopes will be a positive first impression.

Signs of overt sexual interest are indicated by thumbs thrust into a belt with the hands pointing to the spot marked X, or a hand in the pocket, which is more subtly pointing the same way. If you look at advertisements for men's clothes, the model very often stands with one hand in his jacket or trouser pocket. Feet, too, can show the direction a man's thoughts are taking. If he is interested or curious about another person, one or both feet will be pointed in that direction, even if the rest of his body is not. This also applies to single-sex groups, where it will show empathy or interest.

Women also rearrange their clothes and tidy their hair if they are approached by somebody they find attractive; and their feet, too, act as indicators of interest or sympathy. When sitting, they tend to cross and uncross the legs more slowly, especially when wearing a short skirt.

Stroking thighs and pushing a foot in and out of a shoe display quite strong signs of sexual attraction, and both sexes will play with objects when getting to know one another. It can be fascinating to watch couples having dinner, for instance. Either sex can find themselves doing something extremely Freudian with the stem of a wine glass or an unsuspecting saltcellar! Watch, too, how the glass will be subconsciously pushed backwards and forwards as the course of the conversation changes, and the allure ebbs and flows.

THE VOCAL IMAGE

I expect we have all formed a vocal image of someone at some time or another. It might be a client at the end of the telephone or an actor on the radio. Very often the voice and the physique do not match up, which can sometimes be quite disappointing! Chapter 3 looks in more detail at the voice and what we can do to improve both range and expression. The voice is our most powerful instrument of communication, and it is vital that we use it well.

It is important not to speak too quickly. Nerves often cause us to speed up, which can be off-putting for others. It is a good thought to rehearse what you are going to say when you first meet someone, even if it is only 'hello' and stating your name.

You never get a second chance to make a first impression, so remember to:

- Choose clothes suitable for the occasion.
- Stand tall when you enter a room.
- Look the other person in the eye.
- Give a firm handshake.
- Know what you are going to say.

3

building confidence

Confidence is something we all lack at some time in our lives. Even the most assured-looking men are probably quaking in their shoes at the thought of giving a major presentation or facing an important interview. People often say to me 'you never seem to be nervous', despite the fact that I suffer from nerves as much as the next person. I always think of a phrase one of my partners in Public Image uses when advising people on coping with nerves: 'people would worry less about what others thought about them if they realized how seldom they do'. We are all self-centred beings who focus most of our attention on ourselves most of the time.

Having said that, self-confidence is vital if we are to succeed in life. A presentation that failed miserably because your voice faltered and your eye line never left your notes can leave a lasting negative impression on both you and your audience. A boss who constantly checks everything you do undermines your confidence. It is important to analyse why we feel the way we do, as there are different ways of boosting morale.

There are three steps to becoming confident.

1 Facing our fears
2 Gaining self-knowledge
3 Positive thinking

If people are not confident, they have a fear for a specific reason. They may fear that they will be laughed at, that they will look ridiculous or that they are not as good as someone else at a specific task. Whatever your anxieties, facing up to them is vital. Ask yourself:

- Have I always lacked confidence?
- When did I begin to lose it?

Then examine the reasons why it is lacking and look for ways of regaining it. You can do this in different ways:

- visualization
- discarding negative thoughts
- improving weaknesses
- relaxation.

As Lenny Henry says, be positive! Try envisaging the best out of a situation. If you think you are going to fail, you are much more likely to do so. If you anticipate a disaster, there will probably be one. Strive to make yourself look forward to the circumstances, whatever they are, and visualize success beforehand. This technique can be used in every situation, even a confrontation with the children. If you expect to have a problem getting them to do their homework, then you will. It might be naively optimistic in some situations, but a positive focus to your life is contagious.

Getting to know and acknowledge your weak points is also important. You may hate public speaking, but if it is part of your job, make sure you get help. Public Image runs 'Confidence Clinics' and courses on public speaking, as do many other companies. Ask around; badger your boss into sending you on a course; if you are self-employed, seek expert advice.

Situations you are unsure about are sometimes better avoided. If something is very stressful and you know you are not going to be able to cope, do not do it. Face-to-face confrontation might be anathema to you, for example; in that case write a letter or a memo, so that you can say what you mean without feeling you are going to lose control of the situation. Give yourself the time and the environment to think clearly and put your point across. If you find that negotiating is a weak point, write down the outcome that you are looking for and stick to it. If it is a price, for instance, and you are worried that you are going to be beaten down, you might say something like this to your customer: 'I have thought things through very carefully, Mr Wilson, and I do not see any way in which I can lower the price further without affecting the safety of my drivers. I know you would not want me to put anyone at risk or affect the quality of the service which, you must agree, is second to none.' Have the confidence to follow your own judgement. Both positivity and negativity are communicable and pass from person to person. Try to absorb the positive and disregard the negative.

We all have something that perks us up a bit when we are down. If you are feeling particularly apprehensive, give yourself a treat. It might be a splash of your favourite aftershave or buying a new item of clothing or a special pen. Focus on your good points. You can help build confidence by making a list of your:

- strengths
- talents
- skills
- achievements.

These could be in any field, either domestic or in the workplace. I cannot stress heavily enough that everybody has abilities and accomplishments of which they can be proud. Think about yours and focus on them.

PRESENTING A CONFIDENT IMAGE

Dressing with Confidence

If you know you are wearing the 'right' clothes and look good, you will feel confident on any occasion, whether social or professional. But what is 'right?' An outfit suitable for a day at the races might not be fitting for a day watching rugby. Corporate entertaining still plays an important part in making contacts and getting business, so whether you are there as part of your organization or as a guest with a partner, it is essential that you look 'right' if you are going to feel confident. Although etiquette and dress codes are not as rigid as they once were, there are still certain guidelines that should be followed to create the appropriate image. Chapter 8 looks at this subject in more detail.

Speaking with Confidence

Your voice plays a huge part in projecting confidence. A tell-tale tremor can sow seeds of doubt as to the validity of what you are saying, whilst a monotonous drone will turn anybody off. Good diction is important, otherwise people will have difficulty in hearing what you are saying, leading to unnecessary misunderstandings and poor communication. Accents, as I have said, can cause bias, especially if they are very strong; but they should not be a problem unless they are difficult for anyone outside that region to comprehend. Unless you feel that you are at a disadvantage from betraying your origins, I would not attempt to lose an accent. If, however, you feel uncertain because of it, there are exercises and tuition available to help you speak 'standard English'.

Men have far more trouble than women with their voices, and they have to try harder in many cases to make themselves sound interesting. Here are some procedures to improve diction, and help train the mind and mouth to work together at the same speed. I hope these tips will be of assistance in everyday conversation at work or at home, not just when preparing for an interview or a presentation, as good communication is vital to success in any field.

It is important to remember that the sound we hear in our own head is not necessarily the one other people hear. If possible, therefore, read all these exercises into a reasonably good tape recorder (not a Dictaphone) so that you can get to know your voice and monitor the improvement.

All these exercises work on different levels. They rehearse the voice and help you to be more relaxed and confident as well as limbering up all the muscles we use for articulation. They will enable you to achieve strong, clear speech if practised regularly.

Expression

If a voice has no expression, no one will listen to it, no matter how important the message. It is therefore vital that we learn to use the vocal range that we all possess to its full advantage.

> Say aloud: 'That was a nice meal.'
> With more feeling: 'That was a lovely meal.'
> Aim the pitch at the top: 'That was a delicious meal.'

> Normal: 'That was a nice meal.'
> Down in pitch: 'That was an average meal.'
> Right down: 'That was a disgusting meal.'

Another useful exercise is to read a section of the newspaper into a tape recorder in several different ways. As if:

■ You are speaking at a wedding.
■ You are speaking at a funeral.
■ You are addressing a large crowd.
■ You are talking to a group of children.

The same text should sound completely different each time you read it, proving that it is not just what you say that is important, but the way you say it. Try reading this sentence, stressing each word in capitals.

> HOW many people are you expecting?
> How MANY people are you expecting?
> How many PEOPLE are you expecting?
> How many people ARE you expecting?
> How many people are YOU expecting?
> How many people are you EXPECTING?

The emphasis dictates the subtle changes in meaning of the sentence, so analyse the text and stress the relevant words.

If you have young children, tape record the stories you read to them, especially the ones where there are a number of characters, so that you can experiment using the whole of your vocal range.

Breath Control
Breathing correctly is essential for good voice control and production. It is important to practise breathing exercises to develop control over the muscles in order to produce your voice at varying volumes, with longer phrasing and ease of speech. When you breathe correctly for speech, the following sequence of events takes place:

1 You breathe in deeply.
2 The diaphragm (a dome-shaped muscle in your chest) descends, the chest moves outwards and upwards and more air fills the lungs.
3 The diaphragm rises again while the ribs stay in the same position and air is expelled.
4 The ribs descend and further air is expelled.
5 Sound is caused by the breath striking the vocal cords. It is important to try and be as relaxed as possible. Tensing causes the breath to be shorter and the voice poor.

These exercises will help you control and use your breath properly.

1 Breathe in and say the months of the year as you expel the breath.
2 Try humming and filling the resonators in the head so that you can feel the head throbbing.
3 Read a poem or a passage of prose and mark the places where you need to breathe. Whisper the piece, then gradually increase the volume. Be aware of the lips, mouth and tongue. Practise saying words in an exaggerated way so that you can feel the tongue, lips and mouth moving.
4 Now try using these two phrases (take a deep breath before each sentence):

I can make my voice rise higher and higher and higher.
I can make my voice go deeper and deeper and deeper.

This is another exercise to help you control your breathing. Take a breath after every line:

I
I must
I must control my
I must control my breath
I must control my breath and
I must control my breath and sustain
I must control my breath and sustain my
I must control my breath and sustain my sentences

Clear Speech
Repeat each of the following phrases about three times, beginning with a whisper and increasing the volume through the second and third repeats. Do these exercises occasionally in order to increase the agility of the tongue, lips and mouth. Try to keep the words clear and sharp:

Twist the twine tightly round the tree trunks.

Did Dora dare to deceive David deliberately?

Kate Cooney carefully closed the kitchen cupboards.

Gregory Gartside gained good gradings in English grammar.

Naughty Nora has no nice neighbours.

Little Larry Lester lolled lazily on the lilo.

Peggy Babcock.

Red leather, yellow leather, red lorry, yellow lorry.

Unique New York, New York unique.

Fresh fried fish.

A cracked cricket critic.

Try tying the twine round the three tree twigs.

The seething sea ceaseth and thus sufficeth us.

She sells sea shells on the sea shore.

Theophilus Thistle, the successful thistle sifter, in sifting a sieve full of unsifted thistles, thrust three thousand thistles through the thick of his thumb.

How much wood could a woodchuck chuck / If a woodchuck could chuck wood? / As much good wood as a woodchuck could chuck, / If a woodchuck could chuck wood.

Confident Body Language
Stance is vital to portraying confidence. Here are a few tips:

■ Stand tall with your head up. The fact that you are looking people in the eye will help you feel on a par with them.

■ Roll your shoulders up towards your ears and then down until they rest naturally.

■ Pull your stomach in.

■ Tighten your buttocks.

■ Walk with your head up, keeping the weight back, and take steps that feel comfortable – not too long and not too short.

STRESS AND RELAXATION

We all suffer from stress, but it affects different people in different ways. At worst it means days off work or even spells in hospital; at best it makes us feel tired and irritable. But stress has always been part of the human condition. Pain, fear, effort, worry and lack of time are among the many causes. It is impossible to avoid stress, but it is possible to control it using good relaxation techniques.

Relaxation means being at ease, letting go of the tension that often accompanies a busy life. Proper relaxation of both body and mind is essential for health, both in your business and social life. The result is a relaxed, healthy body and a clear mind.

To combat stress try and make more time:

■ for journeys
■ to accomplish tasks
■ for yourself
■ for your family
■ for your friends.

Each day, sit quietly or lie down if possible, even if only for a few minutes, and let yourself unwind. Concentrate on your body, on every muscle, as you feel it begin to relax.

The more you are able to relax, the more you will feel able to cope with everyday problems, and this will help increase your confidence and mental energy. There are many courses and workshops run to help people cope with stress, as well as books and tapes on the subject (*see Bibliography*), so you will probably find something that suits you.

Relaxation Exercises
Here are some very simple exercises to relieve some of the aches, pains and overstretched nerves caused by the build-up of stress. These basic exercises can help get rid of tension caused by the everyday niggles of home or work, which combined with rushed appointments, hurried

deadlines, missed meals and disobedient children can all add up to stress!

1 Stand or sit comfortably and let your head roll round gently at least three or four times.
2 Shake your wrists.
3 Breathe in slowly and gradually exhale. Repeat three times.
4 Tense your whole body, clenching your fists and screwing up your face until you can feel yourself trembling – then relax and breathe deeply in and out to the count of three.
5 Raise your arms above your head and stretch to the ceiling, then drop down from the waist, swinging your arms down and bending the knees. Gradually come up again to a standing position. Repeat six times.
6 Roll your shoulders in a circular movement.
7 Raise your shoulders to try to touch the ears. Hold this position, note the tension and release. Do this five times.
8 Push or imagine yourself pushing against a wall about a foot away at shoulder height. Gradually release the effort and allow your arms to fall to your side.
9 Stand in as relaxed a position as possible, making sure your head is comfortable. Place your hands on your lower ribs. Breathe in through the nose to a count of three, but do not tense and raise shoulders. Feel the ribs swing outwards. Hold for three, then exhale for three. Gradually build up the count.

BUILDING CONFIDENCE IN OTHERS

It is important to help build confidence in colleagues, subordinates, partners and children. Giving people a sense of their own worth enables them to develop their personality, achieve their true potential and work to capacity. To encourage this, strive to:

■ Compliment whenever practicable, on appearance as well as results.
■ Motivate by encouraging new ideas.
■ Criticize constructively, pointing out where things have gone wrong and giving guidance on how to improve them.
■ Praise as much as possible.

As I said to begin with, we all lack confidence at some time, but if you make the most of your good points and recognize the weak ones, you can do much to boost morale. Whatever you are going to do, take time to prepare. As we say in Public Image: whatever the circumstances, preparation is the key to confidence, and confidence is the key to success.

4

what do they want?

This chapter features different organizations and reveals what they are looking for when they are recruiting. Although there is not room in this book to cover every possible career, I have put together what I hope will be useful advice on some of the mainstream career areas, and much of the information is transferable to other sectors. Some of the people to whom I talked are personnel officers or training and development managers; others are those who work in industry or the professions and can give first-hand information as to what qualities are needed for the job, as well as the image required.

For most positions these days, companies have an idea of the image they want for the ideal employee. If that image does not apply to you, then it is fair to say that you are unlikely to be happy working in that organization. How you dress is important, not only for an interview but also when you start the job. You should not try to be what you are not, and if wearing a suit every day is something that will make you feel desperately stifled and uncomfortable, then you should look seriously at an alternative career.

You may think that by dressing in an unconventional way you are showing that you are an individual with an unusual brain, but the message received might be of somebody who is a loner, a potentially difficult person who will not fit in. Inadvertently, you could be giving off all the wrong signals to a potential employer or, if you are looking for promotion, your boss. It is wise to find out as much as possible, as early as possible, about the corporate image. This will tell you not only how you must dress, but also the way in which you are expected to behave and the type of people you will be working with.

There are certain qualities needed for almost any job which employers look for beyond qualifications and a track record. These qualities are relatively easy to identify and there is usually evidence available if candidates have had previous jobs. They are:

- **Resourcefulness:** helps people find ways around problems and seek out solutions. If an employer gives you a project, he or she does not want you to come back every five minutes asking what to do.
- **Resilience:** sees people through in the long term. It is a combination of stamina, being able to cope with the politics of an organization, the capability to overcome barriers and to solve problems time and time again without giving in. Employers need people who are good at coping with change. For management positions, the ability to introduce change is often an asset.
- **Responsibility:** is self-evident from a few well-chosen questions. What do you do in your spare time? What is your position in the family? Have you had to care for siblings while your parents were working? How much did you contribute to the running of the home? All these experiences help mould your character.
- **Vision:** to be successful you need to have vision. Change in management and environment is the norm today, so an indispensable element is the ability to see learning and development as part of your own responsibility. To be curious is part of survival. Never take things for granted and never be afraid to ask the question 'why?'.

Dale Carnegie once said, 'About 15% of one's financial success is due to one's technical knowledge and about 85% is due to skill in human engineering – to personality and the ability to lead people.' John Paul Mitchell Systems Ltd., the hair-care people, have a set of ten points they look for when recruiting. These are an employee's:

1 beliefs
2 values

3 desires
4 drive
5 knowledge
6 eagerness to learn
7 ability to organize and communicate
8 willingness to do more than is asked
9 vividness of imagination
10 approach to exercising powers of choice.

To John Paul Mitchell Systems and many other companies, the right image means having 'poise and taste'.

THE 'PROFESSIONS'

A career in one of the professions – such as accountancy, chartered surveying, insurance, the law or banking – requires particular qualifications and certain qualities. These professions have undergone many changes over the last decade, and competition for jobs is ever increasing. The number of graduates applying for jobs outnumbers the vacancies. Arthur Andersen, the international accountancy firm, can take the cream of the crop as far as recruitment is concerned. It receives about 400 applications for every job. Nevertheless, many organizations say that they have difficulty finding the 'right' people.

So what will make you the right person? Obviously, certain qualifications are necessary. 'A' levels are important as they are the gateway to university. There is a view, however, that they are the worst predictor of managerial success, or even of a good degree. But they are a discriminator, and various companies put a lot of emphasis on them, even when recruiting undergraduates, because they are the most recent difficult qualification they can assess. Some accounting and financial services firms, for instance, tend to look at UCAS points and 'A' levels when recruiting graduates.

Accountancy and Financial Services

To train as an accountant you need a good degree – a first or an upper second. Although it can be in any discipline, employers look for maths 'A' level or give a numeracy test at the interview. They also need people with good communication skills who can handle queries diplomatically and mix with clients. The image of accountants is slowly becoming less dull, and these days people are encouraged to be individual while still projecting the professional image of their firm.

Chartered Surveying

To fill the post of chartered surveyor you would need a degree in estate management or a qualification from the Royal Institute of Chartered Surveyors, which can be gained by correspondence courses or day-release schemes.

You do not have to be qualified to be a residential negotiator for an estate agent. A sound knowledge of the locality, plus flair and personality, good communication skills, enthusiasm and motivation are what is needed to sell houses. The smaller firms are generally looking for someone who will be with them for some time, so loyalty is important. If an employer sees a CV from someone over thirty who has moved jobs a lot, questions as to loyalty and competency immediately spring to mind. If you have changed jobs frequently, make sure you have a plausible explanation. For more on this, *see Chapter 5.*

Insurance

The insurance industry has seen changing fortunes in the last decade. In many organizations, the number of recruits has fallen from hundreds to around twenty per year. In the last couple of years, Royal Insurance has recruited between ten and fifteen graduates for the general insurance training programme out of 600 to 800 applicants. Life is tough!

A great deal of time and effort is put into developing and training managers, so employers are looking for people with vision. A belief that things can be done better and the wish to influence is what they require in a management team, as well as self-belief and belief in the company.

The Legal Profession

To become a solicitor you need a degree. Then there are specialist exams: the CPE (Common Professional Exams) if you have not taken a law degree, and the LPC (Legal Practice Course) required by all graduates. This takes another year at a college of law and is followed by two years as a trainee solicitor. Strong debating skills, enthusiasm, adept use of language and a good voice are useful attributes for the legal profession.

Investment Banking

If you have previously worked in investment banking, employers will want to know about the deals you have conducted, and then about your character. They are likely to ask you about your hobbies and outside interests to see whether you would fit in to their culture.

For most banks in the City, high grades for 'A' levels are required, as well as a good spread of GCSEs. It still helps to have attended a top university, such as Oxford, Cambridge, Bristol or Edinburgh, as the university you study at is considered as important as the subjects you study. This is not the case with the high-street banks.

To work in the City you have to be prepared for long and irregular hours. Most people start between 7 and 8 a.m. and will not go home until at least 7.30 p.m. Getting home at 3 a.m. and working weekends is not unusual, so you will have to be prepared for your social life to suffer, which can mean a fairly lonely life outside work.

Banks such as NWS PLC employ telesales staff to sell their services. This is a difficult and lonely job requiring staying power (working days of between twelve and fourteen hours are the norm) and the capacity to enjoy telesales. You also need a good voice and the ability to project yourself well.

Qualities

- leadership ability
- motivation
- determination
- enthusiasm
- ability to work well in a team
- loyalty
- ambition
- integrity
- ability to work hard
- conscientiousness
- initiative
- drive
- ability to learn a language

Dress

Dress is usually fairly conservative for the professions, although there are exceptions. These dress tips apply to any of the careers highlighted above, or indeed to any office-based job:

- Buy clothes that you can mix and match.
- Choose material that will wear well and does not crease too much.
- Buy clothes that are as expensive as you can comfortably afford.
- Choose sober colours and add a strong tie to brighten things up.
- Try to dress to suit everybody and offend nobody.
- Make sure shoes and briefcases are kept in good condition.
- Remember you are the image of your organization – make it professional!

INDUSTRY

The term 'industry' encompasses such a wide variety of careers that it is possible only to provide general guidelines in this book.

The chemical industry has had a lot of bad press over the last few years, something which it is trying hard to redress. Chemist Helen Sharman was the first British female astronaut, and was launched into space in 1991. Because of her background in chemistry, she was chosen to carry out experiments on protein in space.

Helen feels that many people have the wrong image of the chemical industry and scientists generally. They are frequently seen as grey people who work behind closed doors or in labs. These days, a science degree will regularly open far more doors than an arts degree. A scientific training creates a logical pattern of thought for prospective managers and enables them to look at things objectively, especially when it comes to problem solving.

Telecommunications

BT are meticulous in their recruitment process. They do the 'milk round' at universities and are constantly thinking of new ways to attract graduates. For technical jobs, graduates must have at least an upper-second degree. For a non-technical area, the class of degree is not necessarily as important, and qualities such as innovation, determination and communication skills are also taken into consideration.

When filling in an application form for BT, undergraduates are asked to state the class of degree they are expecting. Most people say they are expecting an upper second, although only relatively few of students obtain one. Be realistic, even if you are anticipating a lower second. If you say you are expecting a first, then you had better be confident, as it would be seen as an outrageous lie if you did not get one! O levels can sometimes be used as a useful predictor of degree results. In the days before GCSEs, ten high-grade 'O' levels used to mean that you were likely to make a good manager; in all likelihood, A levels will predict the same. A broad spread of GCSEs, including English and maths, is essential if you want to work for BT, as well as three good 'A' levels.

Qualities

- leadership ability
- commercial and business awareness
- motivation
- determination
- communication skills
- ability to work as part of a team
- attention to detail

Dress

In industry, how you dress is more important if your role involves customer liaison. If you are in a technical job where you do not really meet the public, dress is not so significant.

THE MEDIA

Acting

The image of this part of the media is one of glamour, high earnings and 'luvvies'! Although it does have its glamorous side (a small percentage of actors do earn huge amounts of money) and its share of loveable eccentrics, the reality is a tough, overcrowded and precarious occupation. That said, it can also be the most exciting profession in the world. If acting is what you really want to do, it is essential to be realistic about both your ability and your dedication. If you are going to succeed in the theatre, for example, it is as well to be able to sing, dance and play at least one instrument as well as act!

Acting on television and in films is rather different from theatre work. Television and film actors have to keep themselves alert during time spent hanging around the set while the crew is setting shots and overcoming technical problems. Once the curtain rises in the theatre, you are on! On stage, you are more or less on your own, but in films and on television, many people play a role in creating the final product. Technicians, the camera crew and other behind-the-scenes staff can all contribute towards you and your performance.

There is no better training for an actor than a repertory theatre company. This gives you the invaluable experience of playing different characters throughout the season. You can also study at a good drama school or take a degree at university. One of the advantages of drama school is that agents and directors go to see the end of year productions to find young talent. If you go to university, do a combined degree so that, if things do not go according to plan, you will be qualified to get another job.

Luck plays a great part in success, as does being in the right place at the right time. With so many actors and actresses to choose from, it is often a case of the face fitting the part. A good agent who keeps his or her ear to the ground as well as negotiating the right deal is also crucial.

When actress Jennifer Saunders holds auditions she generally makes up her mind pretty quickly. It helps if somebody projects the right image and looks the part. 'Some casting directors don't bother to find out what the role is and give the actors no help at all. If they look right it is a great help, as our rehearsal schedule is so fast that we have no time to work on creating the character. I need an actor who is as near that character as possible.'

First impressions are considerable. 'I immediately notice what people are wearing,' says Jennifer. 'I expect them to be presentable. If they can't make an effort for the audition, will they make an effort when they work?' Eye contact is vital. Jennifer herself used to be very shy and found it difficult to look people in the eye, 'Which is probably why I didn't get that much work at one time! But certain things put me off immediately. I won't employ anybody with nose or eyebrow rings on principle.' Never mind the image they are projecting, they make her feel sick!

I asked Jennifer whether her own image had changed with success. 'I think people are more intimidated by me now, and I am unbearably cocky when I go into the BBC!' Age as well as success has brought her confidence. She is certainly in a position to call the shots, but she is entirely sympathetic if people look nervous at auditions, and tries to put them at their ease. She is interested in how they project themselves, and how they react to her.

Be careful which parts you accept. If you say yes to everything, you take the good with the bad. To be selective is a luxury, but it is the right thing in the long term if you want to build up a particular image. Get hold of the script before the audition if you can and work on it. Find out about the director, and discover what he or she likes.

As an actor, you set yourself up for criticism, and some people will try to undermine you. It is difficult not to be upset by gossip and bad publicity, but if you really want to become 'famous' you have to ask yourself whether you will be able to stand the pressure of being public property. You have to learn to expect the worst and yet deal with success. This is something that, unfortunately, is not taught at drama school.

Television and Film

At least 800 graduates apply for every researcher's job at the BBC. A staggering 59 per cent of all students want to work for the BBC! This is typical of the sort of competition throughout television. For most production jobs, a degree is now required, although it does not matter in what discipline.

If you are thinking of becoming a radio or television producer, director or presenter, word-processing skills are extremely useful because many people start off in clerical jobs. Work experience, such as in hospital radio or amateur dramatics, is also helpful. Media courses are not essential as most companies retrain new staff anyway, but they can give you useful programme-making experience.

The film business is also fiercely competitive when it comes to applying for jobs. It differs from television, however, in that new companies tend to be formed for each production, which can take well over a year to complete, so everyone is effectively freelance. The television industry is now heading much the same way, with fewer permanent posts and more and more people being employed on fixed-term contracts. Throughout the television and film industry, the ability to work as part of a team is essential, so a friendly nature is important, especially for anyone working in a small organization.

Enthusiasm is another key requirement. People must be keen, unafraid of a challenge and prepared to tackle the unusual.

'We are viewed as rather glitzy and slightly avant-garde as an industry,' says Geoff Hackett, former Senior Producer for The Executive Business Channel. 'In fact, much of the work is office based, using the latest technology.' Geoff always wears a suit and reckons that it matters to look smart. 'You are representing the company whenever you are out on location, filming in someone's office or interviewing people in the street.'

For the technical posts in film and television, 'A' levels in maths and English are necessary. If you are applying for the job of a camera operator, for example, and you have not worked in this field before, you need to bring to the interview some proof of your enthusiasm and ability, such as a video you have made or a portfolio of photographs. Knowledge of relevant equipment is vital. If you already have some experience in the industry, it is a good idea to put together a short show reel of programmes you have worked on.

If you work for a small organization, the image you present to clients is very important. You might be the only person 'on view' to the customer or viewer. If you present a good public image, you will then be remembered and may be invited back again to film. Even the best camera operator or sound recordist in the world will not be employed by some companies if he looks a real mess.

Journalism

Journalism is another overcrowded profession in which job security is certainly not what it was a few years' ago. Probably the most important quality for a journalist to have is curiosity, followed by the ability to ask incisive questions and the skill to make a story different, to make it stand out in such a way that people will notice it.

If you are at school or college and are interested in journalism as a career, write as many articles as you can for the school or college magazine. Practice does make perfect. Work experience is vital, so volunteer to work unpaid during your holidays for the company you want to work for eventually. This will show the editor that you are really keen. It also gives you the opportunity to get involved, and if you do the job well, there is a good chance of a job if a suitable one comes along as people like to work with someone they know. If you have to earn money, then try to fit work experience around paid employment. If, for instance, you want to work on the radio and you are working in a supermarket during the day, offer to help out at your local radio station a couple of evenings a week, or at weekends. It is hard work, but it will pay off! People such as Chris Evans started this way.

Book Publishing

The publishing industry has changed rapidly since the mid-1980s. Company mergers and acquisitions have created a few, very large publishing houses and reduced the number of small, independent publishers. What was once seen as a 'gentleman's' profession is now big business.

Jobs in book publishing include editorial, design, marketing, publicity and sales. The vast majority of people in publishing are female graduates, and most start at secretarial level and work their way up. Few publishing houses offer graduate training schemes.

If your aim is to be an editor, it helps if you have a degree or special interest in a particular area of publishing. The majority of graduates enter publishing with an English degree, but there are many types of publishing other than literary fiction. A qualification in biology or languages, for example, may help you secure an editorial post with a publisher of reference books. Commissioning editors, the people who think up ideas for books and sign up authors, need to have a great deal of commercial sense, an instinct for whether or not there is a market for the book out there. Bookselling experience can be invaluable for this type of role.

Compared to other media jobs, salaries are low in publishing. Fortunately, dress codes are fairly relaxed. For editorial, design, marketing and publicity jobs, staff are expected to look smart but not to dress formally. The more creative the job, the more liberal the dress code tends to be.

Public Relations and Advertising

Mark Borkowski runs a highly successful PR company in London. Like most employers in this industry, he is adamant that people working for him should not be seduced by the glamour. Mixing with the stars and entertaining the 'beautiful people' is only a small part of the job; discipline and attention to detail are vital when planning a successful campaign. 'Whether you are selling a product or a personality, you are selling a commodity,' Mark told me. 'You have to look at the commodity, look at the market and look at what you want to achieve.'

In this highly creative world, employers are looking for people with imagination, ideas and a certain flair, but the ability to work as part of the team is just as important. So many people want to work in this field that there is the temptation to try for any job in the hope that it will lead to the one you really want. This can happen in certain cases, but if your aim is to be a copywriter and there are no jobs around, do not apply for one as an account executive as the qualities needed are quite different.

Depending on the area of PR or advertising in which you work, you may have to think up ideas for campaigns, buy space in newspapers and magazines, design advertisements, write articles, co-ordinate radio and television commercials, organize promotional events or liaise with clients and attract new business. All these jobs require different abilities. Formal qualifications vary. There are some good PR courses available at universities. Sandwich courses, during which you spend a year working with an agency, are a good option. Leeds, Sterling and Bournemouth universities, among others, offer sandwich courses. But qualifications alone will not necessarily get you the job. You need presence and personality for any job in public relations and advertising.

Qualities for Media Work

- total dedication
- motivation
- energy
- enthusiasm
- curiosity
- word-processing skills
- organizational flair
- ability to work long hours
- ability to cope with the knocks
- observational skills
- ability to deal with people at all levels sensitively but firmly

Dress

- Be tidy.

- Make sure you are presenting a professional image.
- Be creative! It is a creative medium you are working in.
- If you are an actor, look the part!

POLITICS

In some senses, the public image of a politician, whether he be local or national, is the only image of a politician. This is because politicians perform work in public for the public. If you are a national politician, you have a short-term contract that comes up for renewal every five years at the whim of members of the public. How you appear to the voters actually determines your future career.

The public image of politics has changed enormously over the last few years. A generation ago, that image was affected by the way in which politicians behaved in the House and how they handled debates or arguments. Most people formed their opinions through newspaper coverage of what was said in the Commons or their local council chamber, and through a few relatively respectful interviews on television and radio. Now we see politicians almost exclusively through radio and television. The Commons or the council chamber is no longer the fulcrum of debate, and what is said in the House gets very little coverage. Politics is covered by television and radio in a different way to newspapers. People get their news from radio and television, so newspapers have to provide something different, which is why they often go for the more sensational angle. The Labour Party has been more conscious of its image of late, starting with the red rose campaign and the use of the name 'New Labour'.

Of the message you put across on television, 83 per cent is visual and 17 per cent is aural. It is not so much what you say, but the way in which you say it! Giles Brandreth is MP for Chester. 'You have to be aware of how you come across. You may be opening the gates to paradise in what you're saying, but if you look tired, red-rimmed about the eyes, shifty, lacking in confidence with dandruff, that's what the viewers will remember!' His career as a journalist and television presenter has helped him. Being a familiar face, his image has made him more accessible. 'The star performers in any field of endeavour will tend to be individual, with a personality that is different but seems to ring true.' The old line 'once you can fake sincerity you've got it made' does not hold in politics anymore.

To become involved in local politics, good local knowledge is essential. You also need to establish an image and woo the press because if nobody knows about you, no one will vote for you. It is vital to show commitment. Go to council meetings, read the local paper and get to know the party workers, as they are the people who do the groundwork. A local selection committee will certainly not be impressed by anyone who does not find out all he can about the constituency he wants to represent.

Qualities

- commitment
- capacity for hard work
- excellent communication skills
- drive
- energy
- enthusiasm
- listening skills
- ability to work with people
- tenacity

Dress

It depends on the image you want to put across. Wearing a pair of old jeans for a visit to a factory might get you a substantial amount of press coverage, but it could antagonize party workers! The three major political parties in Britain today encourage their MPs to look professional, friendly and caring. So while it is necessary to be smart, a hugely expensive Savile Row suit would be inappropriate on a visit round a sheltered housing unit.

THE HOTEL AND LEISURE INDUSTRY

A hotel's image is vital as it lives off its reputation. Although the image of Holiday Inn hotels in the past was of fast food, chrome and plastic, the acquisition of the Crown Plaza group gave them the high-quality image and luxury end of the market they needed. Holiday Inn work hard to maintain the positive image they have created for their hotels. How? There is a big emphasis on staff training as they believe in investing in people; each room has a comment card and visitors are encouraged to give their opinions on the service and standards of the hotel; and there are two words printed on every door that opens on to the public areas: 'On Stage'. In the hotel business you are as much an actor as anyone treading the boards! However, the brave face must be backed with sincerity. Most of the larger chains run incentive schemes and awards for staff who achieve high standards, and promotions are frequent, but Holiday Inn is the only hotel company to have a specific graduate training scheme that lasts one year.

To work in the hotel and leisure industry, good presentation and a professional image are vital, as well as the ability to stay and look cheerful after long hours on duty. The need to want to serve and help people is fundamental. If you cannot take orders cheerfully and with good grace, then this is not the area for you. The Ritz-Carlton Hotel Company has a chain of hotels in the USA and Australia. It has a specific self-image for its staff whose motto is 'We are Ladies and Gentlemen serving Ladies and Gentlemen'.

On another side of the leisure industry, Virgin Airlines builds on its innovative image which says value for money, quality products and fun. Will Whitehorn is Corporate Affairs Director for the Virgin Group. 'You can't create an image and sustain it for very long if it's not based on a foundation that is real.' In a high-risk, highly competitive business such as air travel, Virgin is flourishing. Its 'quality' image has helped build customer loyalty, which is the key to survival and success. Will told me: 'We have complaints from time to time. Planes are delayed, for instance, and things don't always work like clockwork. But when things go wrong we make sure we put them right as quickly as possible.' The reason Virgin has such a good image is word of mouth. It provides real value for money and the customers come back for more. Its staff are vitally important to maintaining that image. They are highly trained and, because so many people want to work for the company, Virgin can pick the cream of the crop. 'We want people who are intelligent, and who will be nice to people!' says Will.

Qualities

- tolerance
- understanding

- enthusiasm
- excellent communication skills
- willingness and ability to work long hours

Dress

In many large hotels, all employees wear a uniform and have to look smart at all times. It promotes a sense of unity and equality amongst them. The staff at the door and on reception are the first to greet the customers, so the image they create colours the way guests view the hotel as a whole. Holiday Inn have accounts with clothes companies to create a smart, classical look that will not date in a few years.

The same philosophy applies to airlines and many other sections of the leisure industry, whether the dress is tracksuits and trainers or a smart suit. If you are not provided with a uniform, a smart, professional appearance is what will be required.

CLERICAL WORK

The role of the male secretary is still not a common one, but in these days of anti-discrimination and equality, your application for a clerical position would have to be taken seriously. Entry qualifications for clerical work vary depending on the company and the position for which you are applying. Generally, a good range of GCSEs and sometimes 'A' levels are required as well as a recognized secretarial qualification, such as Royal Society of Arts (RSA) level two in typing. Word-processing and computer skills are essential, but shorthand is not used so much nowadays, although it can give you an advantage. You should aim for a typing speed of sixty to seventy words per minute. An understanding of telephone switchboards is advisable. Book-keeping and a knowledge of languages can be a distinct advantage.

A good telephone manner is important, as you are often the first point of contact a customer has with a company. If you are worried that your voice might let you down, listen to it on a tape recorder – practise answering the phone and get used to how you sound to other people. (For more on the voice, *see Chapter 7*.) A cheerful, friendly personality is what employers want, as well as someone who can use his initiative. In all jobs you are working as part of a team, even if you are Personal Assistant to the Chief Executive, so the ability to work in harmony with others is vital.

Qualities

- good communication skills
- ability to learn languages
- initiative
- enthusiasm
- tolerance
- computer skills

Dress

- Wear a suit or jacket and trousers.
- Have a good, clean pair of shoes.
- Keep your briefcase tidy.

SALES

To sell anything, an outgoing personality is important, but brashness is something that should be avoided at all costs. You need to look presentable and professional at all times because if people cannot believe in you they will not believe in your product, whatever it may be. Due to a tough marketplace, the status of the sales representative and sales assistant has grown over the last few years. The emphasis on sales is greater than ever before. You can produce the best product in the world, but if nobody sells it for you, your company will go bankrupt!

If you cannot stand rejection, then think again before entering this tough world. It also requires long hours, often in the car, with sales areas sometimes stretching from Glasgow to Swindon. The rewards can be very high, so whether you are selling hi-fi equipment, double glazing, commodities, stocks and shares, clothes, ice cream or cars, this could be the job for you if you have 'the gift of the gab'!

Telesales

Telephone selling is often used as a stepping stone or as a stopgap until the right job can be found. You need to like the job and love the phone! You also need to prepare yourself for the number of rejections you will receive and learn not to take them personally. Although you need to have drive and tenacity, you also have to be aware that companies receive hundreds of unsolicited calls, so tact and diplomacy is vital.

Qualities

- drive
- motivation
- ambition
- tact
- tenacity
- dedication
- enthusiasm
- ability to handle rejection
- good voice
- punctuality
- 'the gift of the gab!'

Dress

- If you have a uniform, make sure it is always clean and pressed.
- If you do not wear a uniform, a suit or jacket and trousers is appropriate dress.
- You should wear smart shoes and carry a briefcase.
- Take your jacket off when driving and lay it across the back seat of the car.
- Buy clothes in crease-resistant material.

Remember that in any field of work which puts you in front of the public, it is vital to create a positive image for you and your organization.

5

---

the interview

I have devoted this chapter to the interview because the aim of this book is primarily to help you create the positive image of yourself that is going to help you win that job or gain another promotion. But handling yourself well in an interview might also help you achieve the position you want in a voluntary organization, get you elected to the board of governors of your children's school, become the chairperson of your golf club or be selected for the local council.

The information in this chapter should be relevant to anyone applying for a job, whether they be graduates or experienced employees looking for a new position. However, there is some specific advice for graduates at the end of the chapter.

Interviewers make up their mind about a candidate within the first sixty seconds of an interview. How you walk, how you say 'hello' and how you are dressed all help to form a positive or negative image. There are several things interviewers for any position will look out for:

- first impressions
- relevant experience
- necessary skills

- reason for applying
- preparation.

Recognized qualifications may be required for many careers, but for any post, the first impression must be a positive one. The number of applicants for most appointments is very high these days, so you only have a few minutes to make your mark and create a positive image. So what makes for a successful interview?

For many jobs you must look right and have a smart, businesslike appearance. The way in which you dress for an interview should, however, reflect the position you are seeking and the image of the organization. Preparation is all!

A successful interview will flow, and you will achieve a good rapport with your interviewer. A good, positive handshake is vital, but take your signal from the interviewer. Do not proffer a hand unless prompted, otherwise the interviewer may think you are trying to teach him or her manners. Eye contact is also important as we cannot tell what someone thinks or means unless we look into their eyes. They really are the window of the soul, so direct your gaze at the person who has asked you the question when you give your response; even if that person is busy writing notes, he or she is still listening to you. Listening skills are essential for you too; an interview can be thrown off course if you answer the question you thought you heard rather than the one that was asked. It sounds obvious, but it is surprising how many people (usually through nerves) rush into an answer. Listen not only to the question, but also to the question behind the question.

APPLYING FOR A JOB

A successful job application is one that is prepared thoroughly and well presented. Before sending off a job application, you should find out as much as you can about the job and the organization, and make sure your CV and covering letter are maximizing your chances of being asked to an interview.

First, find out the answers to the following questions about the organization to which you are applying:

- What does it do?
- Whom does it serve?

- Who owns it?
- What is its market?
- Who are the key personnel?
- How many people does it employ?
- What is its reputation?
- Is the annual turnover increasing or decreasing?

Armed with such information, your application can be more targeted, and should you be asked to an interview, you will already have a good deal of research about the company under your belt. This information can also help you to decide whether the company is one for which you really want to work.

Next, find out more about the job itself:

- What is the job title?
- What is its purpose?
- What are the terms and conditions?
- How will the job develop?

The company may have a brochure or formal job description it can send you to help you answer the above questions.

The Application Form

Some organizations will send you an application form which may be geared to the job. You should fill this in carefully and neatly. It can be useful to write out a rough version first. Unless otherwise specified, do not send any additional information, such as your CV or previous projects, with the application form.

The Curriculum Vitae

Your CV should not undersell or oversell you. There is no point in painting an unrealistic image of yourself on paper: it might get you an interview but, as soon as you walk in, the employer will know you are not right for the job.

Think of the vast number of CVs a prospective employer has to read through, and make sure yours is neat and to the point. If there are spelling mistakes, most people will immediately dismiss your application, unless you are the only relevant person for a particular job. Only use good-quality, white paper. People spend a fortune on coloured paper thinking it will help their application stand out, but when it comes through on a fax, it is often impossible to read.

Be careful what you put on your CV. Highlight the positive and diminish the negative. If you have three 'A' levels, for example, you should mention this on your CV and list the subjects, but if your grades were low it would be wise not to specify them. Highlight unusual features. If you have walked from John O'Groats to Land's End, say so. Do not just put 'walking' under your list of hobbies.

If you left school early without many qualifications, simply state the years you were in secondary education and then list the courses you have been on since. You might, for example, have been to night school and taken a word-processing course, an extra GCSE or learnt a language. You may have been sent on a presentation course and taken part in various training and development schemes at work. Make another list of 'transferable skills' learnt in your previous jobs. Managerial responsibilities, communication skills or something like organizing the firm's annual outing all contribute to making you more attractive to a prospective employer. Even things like having your own telephone and a fax machine at home can seem very attractive to some employers if it means they can save money on providing them. The competition is so fierce these days that a determining factor could be something as simple as that.

Badly presented CVs:

- are on cheap or coloured paper
- have an indistinct typeface
- list the most recent job last
- do not highlight unusual features
- give too much irrelevant personal detail, such as 'I have three Alsatians' or 'I am captain of the cricket team and play at least three evenings a week during the summer' (this might suggest that you would not want to work overtime).

Well-presented CVs:

- contain no spelling errors
- are short, sharp and to the point (covering not more than two A4 pages)
- are on good-quality, white paper
- have a clear, attractive typeface.

Many personnel people spend no longer than six seconds glancing at a CV so it must be well presented. If possible, it should be typed on a word processor and printed on a high-quality printer.

Age

Should you state your date of birth on your CV? Some companies specify an age range in their job advertisements. This practice can, however, backfire. If, for example, the given age range is 28–36, an ideal candidate aged 37 might be deterred from applying. Before you respond to such an advertisement, ask yourself whether this is the sort of company you want to work for.

If you are older than the top of the specified age range but think you are right for the job, write a really stunning letter to accompany your CV and do not mention your age. Once you get an interview you can make up your mind whether to mention it or not. If you are right for the job, it should not make a difference. Do not lie about your age, however, as it might raise doubts about your honesty in other areas.

Even when employers do not specify an age range, age is still a thorny issue for the job applicant. If you put your date of birth on your CV, a prospective employer will make instant perceptions from it. Age should be a secondary thing, so if you are in doubt, skip it and sell your skills, qualities and qualifications.

Hobbies and Interests

Most people mention their hobbies and interests outside work on their CV. This is a useful way of indicating something about your personality to the employer before the interview and to show that you are a sociable, well-rounded individual. However, you should be careful that what you include is relevant and shows you in a positive light.

Hobbies, sports and previous experience are all important if they add value to the job you are seeking. Involvement in amateur dramatics or being the chairperson of the debating society at university would be relevant to include on your CV if you were applying for a job in sales or teaching, for example, whereas it would not help if you wanted to be a computer programmer. If you are captain of the squash team it probably means you are good with people, but too much activity might say that you have not had time to concentrate fully on your work. Be careful how you word things.

Try and put yourself in the employer's position as much as possible. The company is looking for transferable skills that have been gained from a number of different activities. It is not just the fact that you joined the waterpolo team or were part of a research group that is relevant, but how you contributed. If you cannot give an indication of what these transferable skills are then, in an employer's eyes, you have not gained anything. A good example of learning from experience might read: 'We were on a losing streak and I found morale was getting low. I discussed this with a couple of colleagues and we decided on a new tack which helped us win the next few games/move the project forward.'

The Covering Letter

You should write a covering letter to accompany your CV or application form. The covering letter should be addressed to the person who invited the application and targeted to the organization. A generic covering letter will put most prospective employers off, but one that mentions why you are keen to work for their company would be viewed positively. Use the covering letter as an opportunity to highlight the skills and experience that are relevant to that job. Again, correct spelling is crucial, particularly of the name of the company and the person you are addressing

Here is an example of a good covering letter:

Dear Mr Ronson
With reference to your recent advertisement in *The Evening Mail* for an Administrator, I read with interest that you are looking for applicants with good communication skills. I have enclosed my CV, and would like to highlight the fact that I have spent the last three years organizing a large charity event. During the recession it has not always been easy to drum up support, but despite that, we

have raised more money each year. My dealings with marquee contractors, Portaloo providers and temperamental disc jockeys have helped me learn how to cope with people working in difficult conditions (it is not easy to put up a marquee in a force eight gale!). I feel this has given me an insight into the leisure industry and helped develop my organizational skills.

I very much look forward to meeting you.

Yours sincerely

Graphology

Nobody is employed by a Swiss bank or by Air France, whether as a cleaner or a pilot, without a graphology or handwriting test. Job advertisements often ask for applications to be handwritten. We tend to think that an application form is only acceptable if it is on the word processor, but graphology is becoming more popular in Europe. Although these tests are not necessarily accurate, they are likely to be used more and more, so forewarned is forearmed! If, however, a job advertisement does not specify that applications should be handwritten, it is better to type your covering letter.

THE INTERVIEW

Preparation is the key to confidence and confidence is the key to success! Before the interview, find out as much as you can: who the interviewer is, his or her role in the recruitment process and how long the interview is likely to take. Lana Jeffers is Director of Middleton Jeffers Recruitment Ltd. in London. She told me: 'I get lots of well-dressed, good-looking young men who just sit there and say practically nothing, but because there are so few jobs now, people must make a real effort. If you want to work in the city you must read the *Financial Times* every day. If you want to work in advertising you must read *Campaign* every week. You must convince a prospective employer that you are interested in the industry. It is a total waste of their time to train you for six months only to find that you don't like the job after all.'

To Lana Jeffers, like many recruitment agents, references are very important, and she always checks them thoroughly before sending anyone to an interview. You should give the name, address and telephone number of two referees on your CV, making sure you obtain their permission first. A previous employer is ideal, provided that you were happy in the job, and that some of the same skills are needed in the post for which you are applying. If you do not wish your current employer to know that you are applying for another job, do not give his or her name as a referee. If an interviewer questions this, be honest and say that you do not want to mention your application to your employer at this stage.

Apart from former employers, the best referees are people in a responsible position, such as your accountant or solicitor, or family friends who have known you for a length of time. It is not advisable to ask members of your immediate family to provide references. If, however, you have been working for a family business, the referee should state the relationship and write the reference in an unbiased way.

How else can you prepare for an interview? Do not leave it too late – by the time you are panicking it is too late! Always be positive – you will not be offered a job if you do not believe in yourself. Despite the high numbers of applicants, most companies are still hard pressed to fill places with the right people, so they look hard at anyone with potential.

Spend some time thinking about yourself. Write down three adjectives that you would like somebody to use to describe you after a first meeting. One might be 'enthusiastic'; if so, make sure this side of your personality comes across in your interview. 'Hardworking' might be another; if so, show evidence of a project that you have worked on. Write down other characteristics and see if they match up to the job description.

If you would describe yourself as very ambitious, a small business might not have the scope for expansion and promotion that you are looking for. Make a note to ask questions at the interview about career progression. Write down your strengths and weaknesses and consider them carefully. Can the weaknesses be improved upon, and if so, how?

Dressing for the Interview

It is a sign of disrespect for the interviewer if you do not make an effort to look your best. Even though the interviewer will be aware that you are dressing to impress, the signal you are giving is 'I respect you and your status as an interviewer, and I am reflecting that in what I am wearing'.

What you wear to an interview depends on the type of job for which you are applying. People who work in the media often dress less formally than those in the legal profession, for example. To find out how people dress at the company to which you have applied, you could wait outside the offices at home time or go to a pub where employees of that firm might congregate after work. In some careers, such as social work, casual dressing is acceptable because it is the best way to associate with clients. However, you should still wear something smart for a job interview.

Mary Spillane worked in government and public policy in the USA, as well as in journalism and PR. She felt, as an American, that the British were very different, especially in the field of presentation. She told me: 'This self-denying approach that the British took was charming in Britain, but it didn't travel well in the modern world. Americans are very visual people; they rely far more on visual information than they do on the written word.'

The 'packaging' of people and their image is very important. If you look tired and slightly unwell, your prospective employer might doubt your ability to work hard and do the job properly. Colour is crucial, as it can help you to look confident and healthy, reinforcing the fact that you have the stamina and ability to do the job. Colours also make a statement about your personality, but for interviews it is best to wear neutral colours and more conservative styles, unless you are applying for a job in advertising, fashion or the media. If you sport a beard and wear a loud check suit, the interviewer may think that you may be difficult to handle. Alternatively, it might be viewed more positively, in that you are likely to stand out and make your mark. It depends on the nature of the organization so do your homework!

Everybody is different, so it is important to find out what suits you. Employers are not looking for clones; they want something individual. Individuals contribute; they offer that little bit extra that every company is looking for. For most interviews it is appropriate to wear a suit or jacket and trousers. You should be able to wear your 'interview suit' both at work and socially. If you are going to wear light-coloured suits and jackets regularly, it is a good idea to ensure they do not have to be dry-cleaned as this is both impractical and expensive. Always try and choose fabrics that will look smart and classy with the minimum amount of care.

The Weekend Interview

Some interviews are held at weekends. These are generally residential and often include a variety of activities, some of them outdoors, to try and find out as much about you as possible. If you are asked to attend such an interview, a suit would probably be too formal. So, what should you wear?

Knowing how to dress down is just as critical as knowing how to dress up. Do not assume that you can get away with your own notion of what is casual. Colourful casual clothes are a good idea but avoid anything scruffy. Do not wear your favourite Doc Martens if they have seen better days. Jeans are fine if they are reasonably smart, especially when finished off with a jacket. This type of dress would also be suitable for any training courses you may be sent on. It always amazes me that some men think they can wear whatever they like to courses where the dress is 'casual', even shorts and ripped T-shirts. Whenever you are representing your organization, look the part – you never know who is going to be there.

There is a trend in some companies to encourage staff to wear casual clothes on Fridays. This can be a double-edged sword. Although it gives you the chance to show your personality, your dress can let you down. Remember that you may suddenly have to visit a client or attend an emergency board meeting. But smart jeans and a designer T-shirt or sweater would be suitable, or casual trousers worn with a jumper rather than a jacket. If in doubt, play safe.

Remember the following points about dressing for an interview:

- Each job sector has a personality and a culture.
- Learn about the culture.
- Find out what suits you.
- Find out what colours help you to look as fit and healthy as possible.
- Have some personality in your clothes.
- Dress appropriately.

Interview Techniques

Interviewing techniques vary from company to company. You could be interviewed one-to-one, by a panel or board or by two people. All three techniques have advantages and disadvantages. If there is only one person interviewing you, then his or her likes and dislikes, moods and prejudices have be to taken into account. The panel may be rather intimidating, as can being interviewed by two people who adopt opposite roles to see what reaction they get. This type of interview is often conducted by a man and a woman. The woman usually takes the sympathetic role and tries to put the candidate at her ease, drawing out more information. The man plays devil's advocate and can be quite aggressive to see how the interviewee reacts under stress and how he copes with widely varying behaviour.

Sometimes the people conducting the interview are not properly trained, and this can be an uncomfortable experience. If the interviewer is playing a power game, keep your cool and remember that it is not personal. Another sign of an untrained or inexperienced interviewer is one who asks closed or leading questions in a rather haphazard way, frequently interrupting. Other poor interviewers may do all the talking, not allowing you to get your points across. In such instances, it is difficult to be assertive and make your point without seeming aggressive. If you are frequently interrupted, use phrases such as: 'Could I just go back to ...', 'From past experience I have found ...', 'May I clarify a point you made earlier, because it seems to me that ...'. Keep talking enthusiastically so that your interviewer does not have the chance to jump in until you have finished what you want to say.

A good interviewer should start the interview on time and have your details lying on the desk in front of him or her. He or she should ask open questions that allow you to expand to include the points you want to get across. There is also the 'halo and horns' syndrome to be taken into account: we tend to warm to people who share our own values and views, but good interviewers should be aware of this and disregard it as much as possible. Some interviewers take notes, but there is no need to worry if they do not – it does not mean that you are so boring there is nothing to write about!

Do not lose heart if you are interviewed badly and do not get offered the job. Did you really want to work for that person anyway? Every interview, good or bad, is useful experience. It is a good idea to write down the type of questions you were asked and the reactions to your answers; you can refer to this record when you go for your next interview.

Making a Good Impression

For any interview it is essential to walk in like a winner and put across a very positive image. You have to give of your best, and show the interviewer the most compelling facets of yourself. In the final analysis, it is not necessarily qualifications that will win you the position you want, but personal chemistry and image. When you arrive, chat to the receptionist, and ascertain where the interview will take place. Check your appearance; you do not want spinach on your teeth or a label sticking out of your jacket. Think about what you will say to the interviewer when you meet, mentally revise the research about the company you have done and think about the qualities needed for the job.

If you are shown up to the room where the interviews are being held, try and make small talk with whomever accompanies you, even if it is only about the weather. You never know what questions could be put to the staff to elicit information about you afterwards. A conversation, however trivial, will also help you to relax and loosen up your voice. When you get into the room, sit up straight in the chair and look alert! Most important of all, be yourself, not what you think someone wants you to be.

Take a good-quality notepad and pen into the interview so that you can make notes if you feel it useful. Making a few notes also impresses many prospective employers, as it shows you are taking a real interest. You may also find it helpful to have made some notes in advance to take to the interview. If your mind goes blank, headings help to jog the memory. Jot down any evidence of how you fulfil specific criteria specified in the advertisement. Think of the questions you want to ask and make a note of them, but do not feel obliged to ask something. It is fine to say, 'Thank you very much, but I think you have covered everything I need to know.'

The way in which you handle the interview is very important. This is particularly the case when applying for a different job in the same company as, however well the interviewer may know you, you will not get the job if your interview technique is poor. It helps if you treat the interviewer as if he or she had never met you before, and do not assume that they know certain things about you.

Interview Questions

There are many types of interview question. Some questions are straightforward, others potentially more tricky. If you are asked a difficult question that picks up something negative on your CV, do not panic. Stay calm, be reasonably honest and accent the positive. For example, if one of the questions asked is 'Why have you got such a poor degree when your "A" level results were so good?', the answer might be 'I got to university and discovered non-stop partying, but now I've learnt my lesson.' At least you are showing that you are being honest and have gained something from the experience.

Experience can mean different things to different people, and it is something that is often addressed by interviewers. Someone who has been in a managerial position for eighteen months may be just as capable as someone who has been in the same position for five years. In fact, the former may be better suited, as there is a law of diminishing returns after a certain length of time in a job. If you have been in a job for a significant period, it is important to say why you have stayed and what both you and the company have gained as a result; then say why you are leaving.

Here are some examples of the different types of interview questions you may be asked:

Closed Questions

These are the most difficult questions to answer as they are not designed to allow you to elaborate. They are usually phrased thus:

- Did you ...
- Who was ...
- Which company ...

Leading Questions

These prompt a short or particular answer. Examples include:

- Do you think you ...
- Can you ...
- Are you ...

Open Questions

These allow you the most scope in your answer:

- Why did you ...
- When were you ...
- Where have you ...
- How did you ...

Open questions are the ideal, but if you think you are being interviewed by somebody who is not bringing out the best in you, answer the closed or leading question as if it were an open one. You might, for example, be asked

'Do you think you have initiative?'. Instead of answering 'yes' or 'no', you could give an example of when you have shown this quality in the past, such as 'I do think I have initiative because last year, when we had a small fire in the office, people started to panic, so I sounded the alarm, told someone to ring the fire brigade and then made sure everyone was evacuated quickly and quietly'. Or if you were asked 'Are you willing to travel with this job?', the answer could be 'Yes. I have travelled a lot ever since being at school and always enjoyed the challenge of meeting new people and seeing new places'.

Hypothetical Questions
These are usually phrased as follows:

- What would you do if ...
- How would you tackle ...
- Supposing that ...

Try and answer these questions as honestly as you can and imagine what the ideal employee would do, taking into account the job description.

Questions to Expect
Here are some examples of common interview questions with some ideal answers which you may be able to tailor to your requirements.

Q: Summarize the skills and knowledge you have gained.
A: As senior sales assistant I had to deal with all kinds of queries, from staff as well as customers. I also had to make sure the goods were displayed properly, to handle the accounts and, most useful of all, learn to negotiate with suppliers.
Or
A: As a packer at Jones and Walton I had to answer the phones too. This meant speaking to clients and answering their more simple queries. It has given me a lot of responsibility and helped me in my dealings with people.

Q: What would you consider an adequate reward for your efforts?
(This sort of question is to test you and learn more about your

personality. You will have already found out what the salary is, so quote the figure mentioned. If the company has not mentioned the salary, talk to friends in similar situations and look at other job advertisements to get an idea of the sort of figure you should be expecting.)

A: I would naturally like to be paid the going rate for my services! But more than that, I would want the chance to develop my skills as a manager and expand my knowledge of the industry.

Q: What are your strengths?
(Here you have the chance to talk about the good points that might be listed on your CV.)

A: As you can see, I have had several jobs in the holidays that have helped me understand how a retail outlet works. I have also had to organize people's travel arrangements when I was captain of the hockey team, so I feel I have both the personality and the experience needed to work in the travel industry.
Or

A: I have spent the last two years running the sales team in my last company, and as the product we were selling was new to the market, it meant that I was having to look at new outlets, and also to motivate the staff, who were a little unsure of the strategy to begin with.

Q: Would you say you have any weaknesses?
A: Yes. I would say that I am a perfectionist.
Or
A: Yes. I think I am very demanding, and I expect a lot from myself.

Q: What has been your biggest accomplishment?
(Think of something that you are proud of, either at work, school, college or in sport, but make it work-related.)
I won the Southwest Inter-Schools Public Speaking Prize in my last year at school.
Or
At my last company I helped organize a raffle to raise money for charity. We made over £500, twice as much as had been raised before.

Q: Tell me how you moved up through the organization?

A: I worked hard and really thought about where I wanted to go. I was also
fortunate that at a time when Kidman's was expanding, I was in a
position to head up a new department.

Q: Why have you had so many jobs?
A: Well, after I had been at Wren's for a year, they had to make
redundancies. As I was the last in, I'm afraid I was first out. It was
the same at Charlton's. To be honest, I think I accepted my present
job without thinking it through first. The job wasn't right for me as
it offered no chance of promotion, so I thought it was better to try
and find something that would use my particular skills more
fully.

Q: Why were you dismissed?
A: I wanted a position which would provide opportunities to develop my
career but I found that trying for greater responsibility created conflict.
As you know, job searching takes a lot of time, so it was thought best
(by both me and the company) that I should have the time to
concentrate on finding the right job.

Q: You see this clock on the desk? Sell it to me.
(This question might be asked at an interview for a sales position.)
A: What is special about this clock? Apart from the obvious quality of the
design, its battery is guaranteed for three years; it has a large, luminous
dial so that it can be seen easily in the dark (ideal for an older person);
and it is on special offer – a third off its usual price – which makes it just
£9.99 until the end of the month.

Q: What sort of sport do you like?
(This is asked partly to see if you are a team player, but also to see
whether the sport might interfere with your work.)
A: I like to keep myself fit, so I play tennis at least once a week.
Or
A: I am a member of the local rowing club. We take part in a number of
competitions, but I make sure there is always a substitute, as I would
hate to let them down if I am working away.

Q: What are your hobbies?
    (This question is usually asked to find out more about you, and as
    physical and mental health is high on any employer's mind the answer
    might be:)
A: I like fishing. It helps me relax and often provides valuable thinking time
    if I need it.
    Or
A: I enjoy photography. I travel a lot and meet many people when choosing
    my subjects. It has really broadened my horizons.
    (Both these answers tell the interviewer something positive about you.
    Whatever you do as a hobby, try to relate it to the job you are going for.
    If the job on offer means plenty of foreign travel and your hobby is
    photography, the above answer would tell the prospective employer
    that you would feel at home entertaining clients in different countries.)

Q: How do you organize and plan major projects?
    (A tricky one!)
    First, I would establish what the key objectives are, when the project
    has to be finished and how much money is involved. How I would
    proceed would depend on the nature of the project.

Q: Have you ever had any financial difficulties?
    (Another tricky one, but be as honest as you can.)
A: Nothing my bank manager and I can't cope with!
    Or
A: Yes. I had a problem last year which has now been resolved. As a result
    of that I have ...

Q: Describe a difficult problem that you have solved.
    (If you are a graduate or going for your first job, use an example from
    college, school or home. If you are working, think of a problem you have
    resolved recently. It does not have to be a major one. The interviewer
    wants to see whether you use your initiative and can handle the bad
    times as well as the good.)
A: We found we had a problem with one line of goods. I rang those
    particular customers to apologize, and made sure they got replacement
    deliveries as soon as possible.

Q: Where do you see yourself in five years' time?
Or
Q: How long will you stay with the company if you get the job?
A: I want to be here on a long-term basis. As far as I can see, there are
many opportunities, and as you seem to reward progress, I hope to be
able to learn the job and climb the ladder as other positions and
opportunities arise.

Q: There must have been times when you and your manager disagreed.
Why?
(Here the interviewer is trying to find out if you are difficult to work
with. Unless you had regular rows, the answer might be:)
A: I can't think of a time when we really disagreed. He/she was very good
in that he/she would let me have my say, but we always got on well.

Q: Which aspects of the job description for this position do you dislike?
Or
Q: What are your dislikes?
(The first question is specifically about the job. Having done your
homework, you will know what the job entails. Make it the more
mundane things that do not appeal. The second question is more
general, but angle your general dislikes to the job too, as well as things
like television soaps or whatever they might be. Have a reason for
disliking anything, but do not go into a long tirade!)
A: Filing and photocopying aren't my favourite occupations! But I know
that it's all part of the job, and I never mind doing anything that has a
purpose to it.
Or
A: It really gets to me that we have such a poor public transport policy in
this country. If I wanted to come to work by bus, it would take me over
an hour and a half.

Q: Why should I take you on? Why do you think you will be good at
the job?
A: I think I have the right blend of experience and drive that will make both
me and the company successful.
(Then substantiate the statement with experience.)

Q: You only got a 'C' in English Literature GCSE. Were you satisfied with that?

A: I only decided to take the exam at the last minute, so I didn't have as much time to revise as I would have liked. However, it has given me an interest in literature as a whole, and I find I read a lot more now.

Personal Questions

Personal questions can be off-putting and even offensive. If interviewers want to know too much about your personal life, do you really want to work for them? 'Why aren't you married?' is none of their business, and 'Are you thinking of getting married?' is only really applicable if you are applying to run a pub or to become a vicar, where the parishioners may prefer a married priest.

Never get involved in an argument with a prospective employer, even if you feel severely provoked. The interviewer will be testing you to see how well you react to confrontation and stress. There is no need to show your intellectual abilities by lecturing your interviewer, and avoid being critical of previous employers, as it does not show you in a good light.

Tests

Some companies, such as IBM, ask interview candidates to sit psychometric tests. These are designed to find out more about you and determine whether you are suitable for the job for which you are applying. Some firms also carry out spelling and numeracy tests and use graphology (*see page 74*). Personality tests are becoming more important, but they are very expensive to administer. The Occupational Preference Questionnaire (OPQ) asks job-related questions to select the ideal candidate for the position.

Psychometric tests will help define people fairly accurately. The sort of questions used in the tests might be:

- Do you get angry easily?
- Are you assertive?
- If there is conflict do you move away quickly?

The tests have a built-in lie detector but there is no right or wrong answer. We all fit into a category, and some people have different strengths for different jobs. They are meant to help, so do not be intimidated by them.

Telephone Interviews

Some organizations employ companies to sift through applicants by conducting the first interview over the phone. As you may not be given advance warning of the interview, be prepared. Have any notes near the phone when you start the interview, but make sure the desk or table is clear. It is so easy to be distracted and you need to concentrate harder when there is nobody to focus on. Keep the following guidelines in mind:

- Use the interviewer's name but do not be overfamiliar. First names are usually acceptable these days unless the interviewer uses a title when introducing himself or herself.
- Avoid 'yes' or 'no' answers. Try to elaborate on closed questions (*see page 80*).
- Be brief but factual.
- Ask questions.
- Take notes, if not during the call, then as soon as you put the phone down.

Telephone conversations are a skill. Here are some techniques you can adopt to ensure you are coming across well. Some of them apply to telephone interviews, and others are more general.

1 Listen attentively. The ear you use makes a difference. Use the right ear when absorbing complicated information. This is because it connects with the logical side of the brain (the left side). Use the left ear when listening sympathetically, as it connects with the more imaginative right side of the brain.
2 Listen to the call with your full attention, and try and smile when you speak.
3 If you are expecting a difficult call, take the initiative where possible and make contact first. Get to the point quickly: 'The reason I have called you is because ... '.
4 If you are caught on the hop, call back after checking any relevant facts and information to give yourself time to gather your thoughts.
5 When dealing with complaints, do not take them too personally. Keep calm, allow the caller to voice all his or her complaints without interrupting, and listen sympathetically.

6 If you are complaining, decide first what you want to achieve from the call, such as a refund, an apology or replacement of goods. Never lose your temper!

7 If the phone rings when you have a visitor, either at home or in the office, tell the caller politely that you will ring him or her back. If it is urgent, make the call as brief as possible, and either leave the room, or gesture to your guest that you will not be long.

8 Never ask a customer or client to ring back. If someone has taken the trouble to contact you, then you or your boss should return the call. Business has been lost through this slight portrayal of bad manners!

9 Find out and use the caller's name and take relevant details as you talk.

CAREERS ADVISORY SERVICES

Robin Wood is Chief Executive of Career Movers Companion, a recruitment and advisory company with offices in the northwest of England and in Reading. He helps graduates, people in work and those who have been made redundant to find jobs. Once more, it all comes down to preparation. If graduates come to him with no idea of what they want to do, they are given a psychometric test to identify areas and occupations to which they are likely to be most suited. Then the job of writing the CV and a good covering letter is followed by the search for suitable companies for those graduates to approach.

In Robin's experience, unsolicited CVs accompanied by carefully constructed letters are very successful because there is not the same competition as when a job has been advertised on the open market. There are plenty of jobs around, but you may find that some previously done by non-graduates will be filled by graduates, so be prepared to lower your sights a bit.

For people in their forties and fifties who have been made redundant, the future is brighter than it was a couple of years ago. In 1995, Career Movers Companion found positions for more people in the forty-eight to fifty-three age bracket than ever before. 'There seems to be a move away from the twenty-eight to thirty-year-old who is all whiz kid and MBA,' says Robin. 'Many companies now recognize the value of experience, and there is a feeling that if someone has done a particular job well for three companies, he will work well for you too.' Redundancy is traumatizing even if there has been a substantial payoff, so the effort to re-create a positive image can be hard. When you are in the pit, at the bottom of the Transition Curve, it can be difficult to climb out. Self-motivation is vital, and the most important thing for more mature applicants is to identify transferable skills from the job they have left to organizations where those skills will provide added value. Comprehensive research is essential.

The cost of using a careers advisory service varies, but it will probably be in the region of £350–£500. Some companies charge much more, so ask around. The best recommendation is from somebody who has used the firm successfully. The fee includes constructing the CV, writing letters, researching companies, brushing up on interview skills and, in many cases, counselling. It takes about four and a half months for most people to be 'placed'.

GRADUATES

Q: What do you say to an arts graduate?
A: A Big Mac with fries, please.

This is a cruel joke, but it reflects the fact that having a degree no longer guarantees a job. Not all undergraduates make the most of their Careers Advisory Service (CAS) at university or college. The CAS is staffed by professionals who work closely with many companies. They can offer help and guidance to undergraduates, such as sending them on workshops to improve their interviewing skills.

Many companies visit universities in what is known as the 'milk round'. The first visit is likely to be to a careers fair, where undergraduates are encouraged to ask questions from company reps and find out more information about the company before applying. Interviews then take place before final examinations. If you interview well and are offered a job, it will usually be conditional on the grade of degree you achieve, although you will always be expected to set the best classification of degree you can.

I spoke to David Thomas, Head of Development Training at BT. From the huge numbers of applications that come in, relatively few are selected for interview. Interviewers want your personality to come across during an interview, but they will only see the image that you project. Your personality comes across from the way you answer questions, the way you listen and the questions you ask. The standard question from students is 'Can you tell me more about the company's training and development policy?'. If, however, you can ask a question that shows you have thoroughly researched the company, it will make a much greater impression on the interviewer. For a company such as BT, a good question might be 'My interest is software engineering. Is that likely to be stimulated by the multimedia work that BT is doing?'. This shows an understanding of the nature of the business. The more specific you can be, the more profitable the line of interview will be, as it indicates a focus on the part of the applicant.

It is also important to be well informed, both in terms of current affairs and about the industry in which you are interested. Read trade magazines and try to take a newspaper every day, preferably a broadsheet. The tabloids might run a story about BT, for example, with the shock headline 'Granny cut off in the Highlands', whereas the broadsheets would give you more information. When you are asked at interview 'What do you know about the company?', you might answer 'I was very surprised to learn how restricted BT's licence was when it comes to multimedia provision to people's homes'. That is a good example of the sort of response required.

As well as being interviewed, undergraduate job applicants might be also asked to carry out an exercise. Someone applying for a researcher's job with a broadcasting company might be asked to write a programme proposal, for example. Again, preparation is all. If you are applying to work on a specific programme in any capacity, whether at the BBC or with another broadcasting company, it is vital to have a critical appraisal about it. But be constructive in your criticism, as you have to be conscious that the series editor may be present.

Royal Insurance has put together a profile of the type of graduate that fits into the organization. This was based on previous years' experience of selecting interviewees from the many CVs that arrive at their office in Liverpool. 'We now look for someone with an upper-second degree, with work experience; someone who can work in a team and has been involved with people both in and out of university.' Someone with no interest outside their academic studies and/or no work experience would be precluded by many companies. It is also necessary to understand the relevance of a degree to the work you are seeking; just to have gone to school and then to university is not enough.

SUMMARY

Preparing for the Interview

- Remember – the first process is rejection, the second is selection.
- Know what you are applying for.
- Do not send any projects or proof of work unless requested to do so.
- Fill in application forms properly – do not just put 'refer to CV'.
- Find out as much as possible about the organization and what it does. Use the library, read relevant magazines or ring the personnel department to find out more.
- If information is not forthcoming, demonstrate that you have tried to find it.
- Talk to people who work in that industry to find out what the job entails.
- Find out what makes a person successful in that job.
- Use as many contacts as you can.
- Be honest in your CV – do not build up your experience as the interviewer will see through it.
- Make sure your CV is well presented.
- Have an early night before the interview!

Mistakes to Avoid

- Errors and spelling mistakes on CVs.
- Being late.
- Not looking or being alert.
- Not asking intelligent questions.
- Not thinking things through.
- Lack of preparation

Appearance and Presentation

- Make sure clothes are clean and well pressed.
- Shoes must be polished.
- Hair should be tidy (it is not a good idea to wear too much gel or other styling product).
- Do not wear too much aftershave.

- Be well manicured.
- Take notes in an interview (using a good pen) – it shows you have a real interest.
- Make sure your briefcase is smart on the outside and tidy inside.
- Be aware of your body language and voice.
- Do not be too loud or pushy.
- Give a firm handshake.
- Create and maintain eye contact.
- Be enthusiastic!

giving a presentation

Most of us have to give a presentation or make a speech at some time in our lives. It may be to a handful of colleagues or to an audience of thousands. Whether you are addressing a local charity committee or a business seminar, the ability to put your point across in an interesting and informative way is essential. In today's competitive business world, the man who can communicate with authority and confidence has a great advantage over his peers. If you are asked to speak at a social function, then you are quite within your rights to decline if you want to, but if it is part of your job, you have no choice. Today, making presentations is a part of most people's working lives. It is vitally important to do them well, and those who are good communicators are the ones who will make it to the top.

INITIAL QUESTIONS

Thorough preparation is, again, the key to confidence which, in turn, is the key to success. In order to be able to prepare, there are a number of questions you need to ask yourself before you accept the invitation to speak:

1 Why have they asked me?
2 Whom will I be addressing and how large will the audience be?
3 Where will the presentation/speech take place?
4 For how long should the presentation/speech last?
5 Are there any other speakers?

1. Why You?

You will be asked to speak for a number of reasons. It may be because you are a good raconteur or because you are the expert in that field. The fact that you have been asked to speak should give you confidence. If you are an expert in the area, you probably will not have to do as much research for your presentation.

2. The Audience

Every speech, talk or presentation should be written with the audience in mind. What does the audience want or need to hear? It sounds an obvious point to make, but it is surprising how many people stand up and say what *they* want to say, not what the audience needs to hear! Find out in advance the age group of the audience, whether it is going to be mostly male or female, and the job categories of the audience members. All this information will help you target your presentation appropriately. You will also need to take into consideration the size of the audience. If you are addressing a hall full of people, your tone would probably need to be more formal than with a small group.

3. The Venue

In order to plan your journey, you need to know exactly where the venue is and how long it will take to get there. You should also find out the size of the room. If it is large, you may want to discuss the sound system. Find out whether the room is equipped with everything you need for your presentation, such as a slide projector, overhead projector or flip chart.

4. Length of Presentation

Do not be cajoled into speaking for any longer than your information will allow. It is always better to speak for a shorter time rather than over-run. We all have busy schedules, and to waste people's valuable time is a sin.

5. Other Speakers
You need to know if there are any other speakers and, if so, the subject areas they will be addressing so you can avoid repetition.

WRITING THE SPEECH

There are five essential rules when preparing a speech or presentation:

1 You must know your subject.
2 You must be sincere.
3 You should be convinced that your message is worthwhile and that your audience will benefit from it.
4 You must be enthusiastic.
5 You should be self-confident.

One of the things we all fear when we get up to speak is that we will forget everything, including our own name! With careful preparation, however, we will not only remember everything we want to say, but we will also make sure we give our audience all the information it needs in a logical, straightforward and entertaining way. But allow yourself adequate time. Preparing any sort of presentation takes hours, not minutes.

When writing a speech, always remember the following point:

Write the talk to be said, not read.

There is an enormous difference between holding someone's attention with the spoken, rather than the written word. When speaking to people, we have to use language that is easily assimilated. If our audience has to try too hard, it will switch off. The English language is one of the richest in the world, but we tend to use only a fraction of the words available to us. Although you should not try to sound as though you have swallowed a dictionary, aim to make your talks as interesting as possible by varying the words you use. Whatever your message, make it clear and concise.

The Objective
Start by deciding what you want the talk to achieve. Do you want:

to inform?
to influence?
to recommend a course of action?
to persuade?
to motivate?
to entertain?

When starting to write a speech, talk or presentation, it is a useful exercise to jot down in a sentence the message you want your audience to take away with it. This helps to clarify your thoughts and objective. Here are two examples:

To convince my colleagues that it would save the company time and money to purchase all our paper from one source.

To inform the conference that resources spent on training will increase sales and turnover.

Next, put yourself in the audience's shoes. What would *you* want to know if you were listening? If your brief is to talk about a specific problem, take the bull by the horns and mention it straightaway, telling the audience that you are aware of the problem and stating what you are doing to put it right. If people want a particular answer, they will not listen properly until you have satisfied their needs.

Structure and Content

The following guidelines are for talks or presentations of about ten to twenty minutes in length; anything more than that and you would probably need an Autocue (for more on such aids, *see page 107*).

Start by writing down everything that could be relevant and of interest. Have a brainstorming session with yourself. Once you have decided what is pertinent, write out a first draft. There are several important reasons for doing this, the first being that you are sure of getting the composition correct. It is easy to think that you know what you want and need to say, but unless the talk is structured properly, both you and the audience can get horribly confused. How many times have you heard speakers repeat themselves simply because they need thinking time, or have lost the direction of the talk?

Opening Remarks and Introduction
It is often said that if you cannot remember the introduction, it is too long. This is a pretty good rule of thumb. Keep the introduction short, as its purpose is to grab the audience's attention. A quotation or a startling fact is a good way of getting people to listen to you. However you do it, the introduction is the first step down the road of your presentation, and you must make sure the audience stays with you all the way.

Key Points
For the main part of your speech, try to keep to three or four clearly defined points or subjects. Offer your audience something that they need or want to know. The greatest incentives for any one to listen to you are:

> fear
> greed
> topicality
> sex.

In most presentations and speeches sex usually plays a minor part, unless you are going to tell jokes. Even then it should be used with caution, as you can alienate more people than you amuse! Try to make your information topical and put yourself between the audience and adversity. We are all basically selfish, and unless a point has some relevance to us, we are not interested. For instance, if there is news of a motorway accident, the first thought that goes through our mind is 'do I know anyone who was in the area?'. And if we hear of a massive Lottery win, we will read the newspaper the next morning to see if our numbers have come up.

A key point using the incentive of fear might be:

> The current system will be obsolete very shortly. It will cost a lot to maintain, and the longer we keep it, the more costly it will become. The option I am recommending may seem expensive in the short term; however, I believe that to secure the future we have no choice but to replace equipment that is going to put an increasing drain on our resources.

Now using greed:

This new computer system may seem very expensive today, but the savings made in the cost of man hours alone will mean that it will have more than paid for itself by the start of the next financial year.

And topicality:

As you may have seen in the Press last week, the demand for faster, more efficient delivery schedules is increasing rapidly. We at Post-Haste have to be able to meet that demand, so I am recommending a new computer system to be implemented by the end of next month.

Having made a key point, back it up with sufficient detail to prove it, and try to establish a brief but logical link to the next one. The aim is to lift your audience's interest with each point, rather like changing gear in a car. If you can construct your argument to help save your listeners hassle, time or money, you will gain and keep their undivided attention.

Descriptive Phrases
Who said 'a picture paints a thousand words'? Well, it is absolutely true where presentations and speeches are concerned. Any phrases, sayings, anecdotes or analogies that you can use to illustrate a point are worth their weight in gold. Instead of stating that an object weighs 2.2 kilos, try saying it is as heavy as a bag of sugar. When referring to something 20 metres in height, the description 'the height of an average two-storey building' immediately enables listeners to identify with what you are trying to say. This obviously would not apply if you were giving a technical presentation where facts and figures have to be accurate. For non-technical presentations, further examples of descriptive phrases include: 'the initial expenditure is going to cost no more than the price of an average family car' and 'solving the problem was like trying to stop a block of ice melting. Then we suddenly found the fridge'.

Jokes
If you are good at telling jokes, then by all means include some. Do not, however, feel that you have to be a stand-up comic; a joke that falls flat is far

worse than no joke at all. Bear in mind the journalists' golden rule: 'if in doubt – leave it out'. This also applies to any information you are unsure about.

The Conclusion

This is a very important part of the talk. Summarize the major points, demonstrating that your objective has been met and make sure the audience knows when you have finished. If a speaker constantly says 'and finally' or 'to summarize', the audience will have switched off long before he has! One useful way of concluding is to link back to the introduction:

> I said at the start of this talk that time is the one thing we have, so let us make the most of it. Thank you.

Do not end with an apology such as 'I don't think there is anything else to say'. Make sure the conclusion finishes on a positive note. For example:

> In conclusion, we have at last found the solution to the problem, and now I suggest we put the recovery plan into action without further delay.

Opening Remarks and Introduction
↓
First Key Point
↓
Link
↓
Second Key Point
↓
Link
↓
Third Key Point
↓
Link
↓
Conclusion

Figure 6.1
A diagram showing the basic structure of a speech.

Checklist

Once you have prepared your talk thoroughly, check these points before you begin rehearsing:

Is your introduction interesting enough to seize the audience's attention?

Are your key points in logical order?

Have you linked each key point with the one before it?

Have you kept everything logical and clear?

Do you need any visual aids? Will they help or distract the audience?

Have you involved your audience by regularly using the words 'we' and 'us'?

Have you been positive throughout?

Will the talk meet its objective?

Is the talk written in a suitably conversational style?

Have you removed any words that jar or are repetitive?

Have you told your audience everything it needs to know (not everything you know!)?

Is the conclusion effective?

REHEARSAL AND PERFORMANCE

I would never advise anyone to learn a presentation word for word, but the better you know it, the more confident you will be. Many people like to put their 'bullet points' on cards, but even if you are planning to read the talk from paper or an Autocue, it is equally important to know it well so that you can keep eye contact with your audience.

One of the best ways to rehearse is to record what you are going to say onto a small tape recorder (not a Dictaphone). It is only by hearing what you plan to say, that you can be sure you are not using the same 'pet' words time after time. Make the first recording to check the content, and when you are sure that it is right, record the talk again for delivery. Only by listening can you make certain the message you are trying to convey is clear and to the point. Practise reading the talk in front of a mirror. If you have access to a video camera, so much the better. It is the best learning tool for presentations that I know.

You should always stand when giving anything but a very informal talk. If you are standing, the members of the audience have to look up to you, which gives you a psychological advantage. Even in informal meetings it is a good thing to stand up, as it will help overcome the natural vulnerability that we all feel when we are the focus of attention.

But the focus of attention is what you need to be. In order to get people to listen to you, their whole attention should be focused on you. When you stand up to speak, pause, look round the room and smile! A smile does two important things: it creates a bond with your audience, and relaxes the muscles around the mouth, enabling you to use it properly. Start speaking slightly more slowly than usual, and with your voice at a slightly lower pitch. This is because nerves tend to make us speed up or use the voice's higher register.

If you have a sudden cold or sore throat when you are about to make an important presentation, 'Vocal Zones' are used by many actors and singers (including Cliff Richard) to aid the voice. They are available at smaller pharmacies and health food shops.

It is not always what we say, but the way in which we say it that makes people retain the message. There are three important elements to bring to any presentation – the three 'e's: energy, enthusiasm and enjoyment.

1 **Energy** comes from knowing what you need to say and wanting to say it.
2 **Enthusiasm** – If you are not enthusiastic about your subject, then why should anyone else be?
3 **Enjoyment** comes from having prepared thoroughly, so that you look forward to imparting the information.

Body Language

Once more, body language is important. Swaying, coughing, wringing the hands or any other diverting mannerisms act as a distraction. Stand with one foot slightly in front of the other as this helps you to keep reasonably still. However confident your voice may sound, you will appear neither confident nor competent if you are weaving like a snake in front of your audience. Remember, you are the expert when the spotlight is on you, and your audience needs to be able to trust in your ability to deliver whatever it is that you are trying to sell them. This could be a product, a service, an idea or yourself. Whatever it is, you have to put the message over in an interesting, informative and dynamic fashion.

Mannerisms to guard against include:

shifting from foot to foot
rubbing the nose or eyes
wandering around
wringing the hands
fiddling with cuffs
stroking the cheeks or chin.

All these characteristics are tell-tale signs that you are not as confident as you would like to be, so try to avoid them. Eye contact is essential if you are to know how your audience is reacting, so try to look at each member of the audience at some time during your presentation. The old directive that suggested a speaker looked at a spot just over people's heads has been updated, thank goodness! You should be able to control your audience like a conductor governs an orchestra, building them up and letting them down to keep their interest and attention.

There are eight pertinent points that help the delivery of a speech:

1 Pace – variations of speed.
2 Pitch – not too high or low. Feel comfortable.
3 Phrasing – think about what you are saying. Emphasize stress points.
4 Projection – not shouting. Produce your voice with plenty of controlled breathing.
5 Pause – very important. It gives your audience a chance to absorb what you are saying.
6 Posture – relaxed and upright. It is not only important for good appearance, but is also essential for correct breathing.
7 Preparation – fundamental.
8 Practice – it really does make perfect!

Delivery Self-check
Use the following checklist when practising your delivery:

Was my purpose fulfilled? Did I impress, inform, convince?
Was my message clear?
Was my subject well rehearsed?
Did I complement the other speakers?
Was my voice enthusiastic?

Did I come across sincerely?

Were my pauses used to good effect?

Did my face show my feelings?

Were my introduction and conclusion effective?

Did I look natural?

Was the rhythm of my speech good or was it inconsistent or monotonous?

Did I speak too slowly or too quickly?

Taking Questions

When you answer questions, usually at the end of your talk, your presentation is not over – you are still 'under the spotlight'. A positive ending to a talk might go like this:

> I have given you all the information we have to date, so are there any questions?

This is a time when you can expand on some points, but do not let yourself be dragged into a debate with one particularly verbose or disgruntled individual. If you are addressing a large gathering, it is a good idea to repeat the question so that the rest of the audience is sure what has been asked. As you start to answer, look at the person who has voiced the question, and then start to take in the rest of the room. If someone is very persistent and will not let a subject go, you could reply thus:

> As we have not got too much time I would like to move on, but let's meet afterwards so that we can get to grips with your specific problem.

REPEATING THE TALK

Once you have given a talk, you will probably use it again many times, but adapted for different audiences. It is most important to revamp your talk for each audience. This does not take much time and you will get a much better response.

When adapting a talk, it can help to work through the following points:

What part will your talk play in the event, meeting or conference?

Are there any other speakers?

Has the objective changed? If so, write out a complete sentence that describes it.

Think carefully about the people who will comprise your audience.

Write down what your audience will need to know and want to hear.

Check that your introduction is still appropriate and change any key points to suit this group.

If possible, introduce a local aspect or something particularly relevant to the audience.

VISUAL AIDS

The visual aid is there to help the audience comprehend the message, and it should not be used as a prompt for the speaker. How many times have you seen people talking to the screen, sometimes completely turning their back on the group they are addressing? Having said that, speakers (and their audiences) find that slides enliven a presentation. Graphs, charts and diagrams can be used to explain complex ideas and information. Text slides emphasize the structure of a talk and lead the audience through the points the speaker wishes to cover. Illustrations used during a speech tell a story without the speaker having to give complicated information, thus reinforcing ideas and helping audience involvement.

The Secret of Good Slides

There is really only one secret to good slides and that is simplicity. Each slide should be used to make one point only. Slides which contain too much information or illustration look cluttered and are difficult to follow. Too many words make the text small and difficult to read. As a general guideline it is best to have only six lines of text per slide and six words per line. Graphs and diagrams should be similarly uncluttered. If you feel that it is really important for your audience to have information in the form of complicated tables or diagrams, it is better to give them a hard copy in their conference papers.

For an average presentation of forty to forty-five minutes it is most effective to show approximately one slide every two minutes. This does not mean, however, that you have to use twenty slides, but more than this number would probably be too many for your audience.

To prepare for using visual aids in your presentation, ask yourself the following questions – the same principles apply to using flip charts, overhead projector (OHP) transparencies and 35-millimetre slides:

What facilities are available at the venue?

How big/dark/light is the room?

How much time and money is available?

At which points of the presentation will visual aids be used?

Will they be used again? (If so, store them carefully in a box or envelope.)

What is the message you want your slides to convey?

Is it best conveyed in words or pictures?

If the information is very technical, would a handout be better?

Guidelines

OHP transparencies should be computer generated wherever possible.

Use no more words per slide than you can write on a T-shirt.

Do not display tables of figures – convert them instead into graphs, pie charts or histograms.

Use colours – choose contrasting ones and not too many.

Use big, bold letters, whether they are handwritten or typed (5 millimetres for flip charts, 1–2 millimetres for OHP transparencies).

Do not use fine OHP pens.

Leave a border around the transparency – do not write up to the edge.

Mounting the transparency will help ensure it is straight on the OHP.

You can also use the mounts to make useful notes.

Use symbols instead of words sometimes.

Cartoons carry a lot of impact as the audience is more likely to remember something humorous.

Select information – highlight key words in bold or coloured pen.

See how the transparency looks when projected and make any necessary changes.

By laying one transparency over the other (overlays) you can gradually build up information. Overlays should always be well mounted.

Masking allows you to reveal one idea at a time so the audience is not distracted. It is much safer to attach masks to the mount rather than using a sheet of paper which invariably slides off.

Give all your slides a final check on the OHP before the presentation.

Using Visual Aids

Make sure that the audience can all see the display. It takes some practice to use a flip chart or an overhead projector properly.

Overhead Projector (OHP)

A pointer is a useful device when using the OHP. Point on the glass rather than at the screen if possible, as this will stop you being tempted to turn your back on the audience. Stand to one side and keep your eyes on the people you are talking to, checking from time to time that the acetates are straight. Continue talking when you change them so that you do not break the flow of the presentation.

Flip Chart

When writing on a flip chart, wait until you have finished and turned to face the group before continuing.

Slide Projector

It is advisable to become familiar with a slide projector before using it, and to rehearse if someone else is going to change the slides for you. As before, stand to one side and talk to your audience. The screen is not interested in anything you have to say!

Handouts

Any information that needs time to be assimilated should be given out in written form after the presentation. If it is waiting on the seats, your audience will be reading it rather than listening to you. The only exception is at large conferences where the speech is printed in order that the audience can follow while it is being read. Personally, I do not see the point of this. There is no incentive for the speaker to 'entertain' an audience if it is reading every word, and this gives rise to boring presentations. If the text is available as a handout afterwards, it allows ample opportunity to go over any points that might have been missed.

Autocue

The Autocue is a marvellous invention! Teleprompter, the version used in television studios, has transformed newsreading and presenting, and it is now being used widely on the conference circuit. It consists of a small glass screen attached to a lectern which displays the text to the reader but not the audience. The operator needs to see the script beforehand in order to type it into the machine, unless you provide a disk. Then he or she should run it according to your reading speed.

It is essential not to ad-lib! My boss at the BBC used to say that the only good ad-lib was a rehearsed ad-lib, and it is certainly true in this case. If you digress from the script, the Autocue operator will have no idea where you are, and this can lead to all sorts of trouble.

CHECKLIST

Photocopy this checklist and work through it while at the planning stages of every presentation you do:

number of people in audience	☐
ages of audience	☐
sex of audience	☐
job categories/levels of audience	☐
reason for attending	☐
audience attitude	☐
handouts	☐
seating arrangements	☐
visual aids	☐
microphones	☐
starting and finishing times	☐
catering arrangements	☐

7

vive la difference!

Over the last fifty years, differences in the way in which men and women work, dress and behave have been diminishing. Working practices, hours and wages now tend to be similar for both sexes, and the equality women have striven for is almost here. These days, your boss is as likely to be female as male, but how many men would be happy to move abroad because their wife's job took her there? Are men happy to change roles and allow women to be breadwinners, make fundamental decisions and put their career first? If so, what effect has this had on men's attitude to women? These are all questions that will have to be dealt with over the next few years.

ASSERTIVENESS

There is a big difference between being aggressive and being assertive. Assertiveness helps us become more confident about ourselves and in our relationships with others, both socially and in the workplace. Being assertive is about focusing on the specific results we wish to achieve while maintaining flexibility in the way we achieve them.

Assertiveness means standing up for your opinions and beliefs without denigrating those of others. Everyone has a right to an opinion, and it is important to state yours clearly and explain why you hold it. You will sound more confident if your convictions are based on rational, researched arguments rather than emotions or feelings.

Be clear about what you want to say. If you sound unsure, nobody will believe you and you will lose credibility. Using phrases such as the following will help:

- ■ 'This is how I see the situation ... '
- ■ 'This is what I believe and why ... '
- ■ 'This is what I want and why ... '
- ■ 'In my opinion we should do x, y and z, and if we do, the outcome will be ... '

AGGRESSION

An aggressive man will not make a good manager. If you tell, rather than ask, people to do something and rule the roost with a heavy hand, life will not be easy for anyone.

The iron fist in the velvet glove is a better approach. It is important not to be a pushover, but listening is a great skill, and one of the most significant in people management. Examples of an aggressive stance might be:

'Get this into the post by five o'clock.'
'Don't argue! The reason we are going to proceed this way, is because it is the best way.'
'There will be a departmental meeting this afternoon – be there!'

Rather than:

'Could you make sure this gets into the post by five o'clock? Thanks.'
'I can see you have a very good point, but the reason we are going to proceed this way is because I feel it is the best strategy for the whole department.'
'There will be a meeting at two o'clock. It is important, so I look forward to seeing you all there.'

These examples may seem painfully obvious, but can you honestly say you have never spoken aggressively under duress? I know I can't.

MEN AND WOMEN

How has women's changing role in the workplace affected men's attitude towards them? As they are not now so dependent on men, women are marrying later, if at all, and having children later too. The roles for some men and women have completely reversed, with the husband or male partner staying at home to look after children while the woman goes out to work.

Most young women today expect their partner to share household tasks and take an active role in bringing up any children. Older women, however, sometimes find it difficult to come to terms with this shift in emphasis. Those who have been brought up to look after a husband and family as part of their duty find it almost impossible to delegate the chores, and often end up doing everything themselves, even if the husband has retired or is not working. A helping hand without being prompted will go a long way in cementing relationships and improving mutual respect. It strikes me as grossly unfair that some women have to work as well as run the home, and get little or no support from their partner.

CHILDREN

It also seems unfair that, while it is acceptable for men to talk about their children at work and be seen to take an active interest in their welfare, women hardly dare mention them, and would rather say they are leaving early to go to the dentist than admit there is a sick child at home. The father's role in bringing up children is crucial, as they need a role model for both sexes. Try and make as much time as you can to spend with your children. Money and the latest rollerblades or computer games are all very well, but they do not make up for 'quality time'.

If your job takes you away a lot, or you have to leave the house before the children are dressed and do not return until they are in bed, make extra time at weekends. As they get older, make sure you eat together at least one night during the week as well as at weekends. This will enable you to discuss any problems and keep up to date with ever-changing friends and hobbies. If your wife or partner bombards you with domestic issues as soon as you walk through the door, try and be patient. They may seem trivial compared to the mega-deal you are negotiating at work, but they are important to the family unit, of which you are a vital part. Listen to her over a quiet drink, if that is possible in a house full of children! Make time for each other. It is so important not to lose sight of the support couples can give one another if they work together, respecting their different roles.

If your partner is also coping with a hectic schedule, put yourself in her place. How do you like to be treated when you get in from work? If you like the fridge full, the washing and ironing done and a meal on the table, so does she! Bathing the children while she cooks, or reading them a bedtime story can be a great help; and because she probably gets no more time with them than you do, take it in turns.

HELP IN THE HOUSE

For a man bringing up children on his own as well as coping with a hectic business schedule, maintaining the right image can be a problem. Finding appropriate support is vital. If you need help to iron your shirts and organize the children for school, you will probably need someone living in. On the other hand, you may prefer to take your children to a childminder. There are a number of childcare options listed below. The most important thing is for you to feel happy and relaxed so that you can continue to function properly at work. You cannot do this if half your mind is worrying about whether there are clean clothes for tomorrow, or who is going to collect the children from school.

Finding appropriate help can be a problem. When you employ someone, it is essential to define the job, responsibilities and the degree of discipline expected right at the start, then everybody knows where they stand.

Au Pairs

Au pairs are young people, usually female, from abroad who are employed in the home to help with childcare. They tend to live with you as part of the family, and only expect to do a limited amount of housework. They need time to go to college, as they are primarily in this country to learn English. Salaries vary, but £30 a week with free food and accommodation is currently around the norm. Check with friends or an agency to get an idea of suitable hours.

You can employ au pairs through an agency (they are listed in *The Lady* magazine, local papers and telephone directories), or you might find one through friends or business contacts. When selecting an au pair, it is important to make sure that she speaks at least some English. When you are about to dash out to work, it is very wearing to be met with a blank stare after you have slowly and carefully given instructions about the children's tea for the tenth time. It is essential to take up references, and not just from an agency. Try and speak to families for which the au pair has worked in the past. Be sure to explain to the au pair that there will not be another woman in the house, as some younger girls may be alarmed by this.

If it is the au pair's first job, and your work means you are going to be out all day, choose somebody who is not too young and has younger brothers or sisters, so that she has some experience of coping with children. Children can be very cruel, and as soon as they realize a girl cannot understand what they are saying or is too shy to exert any influence over them, they will run rings round her! You should also ensure that the au pair gets used to being in the car with you before expecting her to drive the children, especially if she has never driven on the left before.

Mother's Helps

Many of the guidelines given above for hiring an au pair also apply when taking on a mother's help (perhaps, these days, the term 'parents' help' would be more appropriate). Although a mother's help may be as experienced as a qualified nanny, she will not necessarily have any qualifications and may be quite young. Like the au pair, the mother's help's main role is to look after the children, although she will also help with the housework. Unlike the au pair, mother's helps tend to live locally and to arrive at your home daily rather than live in. Again, wages, hours and duties should be ascertained from agencies and sorted out at the interview stage, and you can expect to pay around £150 a week.

Nannies

Nannies are qualified professionals trained in childcare. They may have graduated from training schools such as Princess Christian or Norland Nannies. The recognized qualification is the NNEB (National Nursery Education Board) certificate.

A nanny's job is specifically to look after the children, but that includes doing their laundry, keeping bedrooms and playroom clean and tidy and cooking and supervising the children's meals. Live-in nannies will expect a pleasant bedroom equipped with a television and perhaps a hi-fi, and probably the use of a car. A good nanny is worth her weight in gold because you know that she is thoroughly responsible and will bring up the children to a high standard. Good nannies do not come cheap, however. The average weekly wage is around £150 to £250 a week plus board and lodgings, depending on the area and their duties. Some nannies 'job share' these days, working for more than one family, so it is worth asking around. It is advisable to have accident insurance to cover your nanny, but she is responsible for insuring her belongings. Contact your local authority for the latest advice.

Day Nurseries, Childminders and Crèches

Day nurseries are run both by local councils and, increasingly, by the private sector. If your working hours tend to be standard, a nursery can be a good childcare option, but if you have to work late regularly, you may have problems collecting your child at the end of the day. Try and find a nursery that is most conveniently located for you.

Crèches work on the same principle as day nurseries but tend to accept younger children. If you are lucky, your company may run its own subsidized crèche. Childminders are usually self-employed mothers who will look after up to five children (including their own). They have to be registered by the local authority, which requires a police check of their home. Childminders will take babies as young as a few weeks' old, and so will some crèches, but the average age of children starting childcare is around eighteen months to two years. Some establishments educate the children gently; others just encourage them to play. Prices vary from area to area.

When choosing childcare, the most important factor is your child's happiness. You can tell whether children are happy with your choice by what they say about it, and the friends they make. Local papers and directories will give names and numbers of childcare facilities, but do go and see them a number of times before making your decision. The best recommendations come from children themselves, if they are old enough, and from their parents if they are not.

Whichever option you choose, try and give yourself enough time to get ready in the mornings so that you all have a good start to the day. At night, put out your child's clothes and your own.

MAN ABOUT THE HOUSE

Redundancy is a traumatic experience for anybody, but worse for the male whose traditional role is as the provider for his family. Losing status often means losing self-respect, so men need to feel that they still have a worthwhile role to play.

The writer and broadcaster Penny Junor and her husband James Leith have four children ranging from seven to twenty-one. When their first child was born, Penny gave up work as a journalist to become a full-time mother, while James continued his acting career. Due to the nature of his work, he was often at home, so he was always an active father. Penny began writing again and this began to snowball until she was working almost full time. Then television beckoned, which meant she was working away from home.

By this time, James had realized that he was never going to make his fortune in the theatre, so he went back to college and did a degree in business management. 'The government were only too keen to pay an unemployed actor to do something useful like learning to run a business!' He became a partner in a company running a chain of pizza restaurants (as his sister is the cookery expert Prue Leith, I suppose it is in the blood) before running his own restaurant in Battersea.

After the lavish heydays of the 1980s, however, came the depressed 1990s, and James realized that the new restaurant he had started could no longer afford to support either him or his partners. At the time Penny had been asked to write the biography of Prime Minister John Major. It had to be done very quickly so James offered to look after the four children, leaving her free to write. That was in 1992, and the arrangement has continued ever since. In fact, it has worked so well that James has written a book about his experiences called *Ironing John (see Bibliography)*.

James believes he has a positive mental attitude to whatever he does, and thinks that having been an actor, a restaurateur and a business consultant means that he has never actually seen himself as fitting into a particular slot. 'The problem with some men who have spent the last twenty-five years climbing the corporate ladder is that they think of themselves in terms of what they do, rather than who they are. I have never had that sort of CV, so I think of myself in terms of the family rather than a specific career or job.' For this type of fundamental role reversal to work, the relationship must be sound and the people involved secure in themselves.

A woman who makes a big deal of doling out money to a husband at home will be undermining him unnecessarily. This will be counter-productive for the whole family. If a man or a woman is made to feel that looking after home and children is a second-class priority, then the children are the ones who will suffer. For a man (or a woman) to be given 'housekeeping' in a way that depletes self-esteem is a recipe for disaster. It devalues the vital role that one partner has to play in order for the household to function successfully. James Leith was once asked in a radio interview whether he minded 'sponging off his wife'. His reply was that children are a couple's responsibility and it is up to both parents to provide for their children's welfare. He then asked the presenter whether his own wife worked. When he answered no, James asked if he thought of her as a sponger – the interview was cut short when the man did not reply. For any woman, the piece of mind knowing that the children are being looked after by their father rather than a nanny, no matter how marvellous, is tremendous. When she is at work she knows that they are in the best possible hands.

In these days of equality, couples will decide who is going to progress faster up the career path and therefore earn more, and that partner will be the main breadwinner. If that is the case, couples have to make allowances for each other, and ensure they both have time to enjoy the children as well as benefiting materially. A working woman who is earning more than her husband should be careful not to cut the ground from under his feet. Recent changes in the workplace have happened so quickly that men have not had time to come to terms with the fact that their partner might be earning more than they do. It is important for the partner who stays at home or is earning less to be given the same respect as the breadwinner.

If it is part of your role to clean round the U-bend, and your partner comes home and immediately starts cleaning the loo, do not look upon it as a criticism – it is not meant to be. Most women still see it as their job to look after the house, and men clean in a different way from women until they have had a bit of experience. They tend to do things one at a time, very thoroughly, so it usually takes much longer. The children may not have been collected from school and the dog may not have had its walk, but at the end of the day there is a very clean cupboard!

Women know that there are certain things that have to be done in a day, and tend to have several jobs on the go at once. This, in fact, is excellent training for the workplace. Large organizations, such as Microsoft, are increasingly looking for the sort of transferable skills that women at home perform every day. Doing the laundry, polishing the furniture, arranging dental appointments and preparing the dinner (to name but a few of the myriad household chores that women do automatically every day) enables them to become experts in time management, flexible working hours and organizational skills. For men to be able to think laterally in the same way can be a great advantage. Most senior managers of large retail organizations are men who rarely, if ever, go shopping with two or three young children; are they the best people to decide on the store layout and staff deployment, for instance? When applying for a job, domestic experiences should be born in mind. Do not be afraid of the gap in your CV if it meant you were busy at home learning transferable skills that will make you a more tolerant, flexible, imaginative and organized manager.

For men left at home, life can be quite lonely. Women chatting at the school gates about fashions and facials do not want them butting in, and men cannot really join 'ladies' lunches' which help pass the time between housework and school-runs for many mothers. (You will often find, however, that working mums are only too pleased to come over and chat, as they do not fit into the 'Gold Blend and gynaecology' set either!) Fulfilling the conventional woman's role can leave some men feeling like part of an alien race. If your husband or partner is running the household, it is important to encourage him to have an outside interest, as well as trying to include him as much as possible in any decision making.

If you do not have a career these days, it is easy to feel insignificant. As most people realize, however, bringing up a family is one of the most important jobs you could have, and that is how you should look at it. It is important, though, not to lose touch with what is going on in the world.

Improving Your Knowledge Base

There are various courses on offer at colleges all around the country. Being able to have a lively discussion about nuclear energy over the dinner table with your progeny can be very stimulating! You might enjoy learning another language, improving your culinary skills, shooting, sailing, golf, painting, pottery, even sitting GCSEs or 'A' levels. Learning a sport with the children is beneficial to all concerned, and the other parents you meet are usually very interesting. If the idea of attending classes does not appeal to you, The Open University runs correspondence courses in a wide range of subjects, as do numerous other organizations.

Even if you only read the newspaper every day (preferably one of the broadsheets) you will keep yourself abreast of current affairs. Reading the financial pages will enable you to join in discussions regarding business matters when you join your mates for a drink in the evening.

ANTI-STRESS BREAKS

For men wanting to create a positive image, it is a good idea to take a break that will really recharge the batteries.

Health Farms
Health farms used to be the domain of overstressed, overweight businessmen. Now, people from all walks of life are finding that the massages and other treatments on offer are a real boost in a busy schedule. They are priced from around £90 a night, and most have special offers. I have listed details of a few below.

Champneys Health Resort
Wiggington, Tring, Hertfordshire
This is one of the most famous health farms. For a minimum two-night stay, it will cost between £300 and £1,000, depending on the room.

Forest Mere Health Hydro
Liphook, Hampshire
This is ideal for those who prefer quality rather than quantity, and a more serious attitude to health. Prices from around £250 to £450 for a minimum three-night stay.

Hoar Cross Hall Health Spa
Yoxall, Staffordshire
Hoar Cross also operates as a corporate conference centre, which might be

very useful when organizing an event to mix business with pleasure. Minimum two-night stay starts from £200.

Shrubland Hall Health Clinic
Coddenham, Suffolk
The accent is very much on health, fitness and diet, and the clientele is slightly older than average. A three-night stay costs from around £390.

Stobo Castle Health Spa
Peeblesshire, Scotland
There is a lovely, friendly atmosphere in this beautiful Scottish castle. It has under fifty guests and is known for its generous treatment package and marvellous food! A two-night stay costs from around £280.

These are just a few of the options, and there are now more establishments opening in the provinces, so it is a good idea to find out what is on offer in your area. Health clubs and gyms are part of most good hotels these days. If you feel you could do with a tone-up, a sauna and a spot of massage, remember, a spot of pampering does a huge amount to boost the ego as well as the batteries. Do not think of it as a luxury, but more as an investment in your most powerful weapon – you!

8

manners maketh man

'Misunderstandings don't exist, only the failure to communicate exists'
(Southeast Asian proverb). Misunderstandings can often be misinterpreted
as bad manners, so it is important to get the communication right. But what
are manners today, and do they matter?

Good manners are an essential part of a positive image. Before
attending a business or social engagement, preparation is vital. Find out as
much as you can about the place you are going to, the people who will be
there and what is expected of you. It is a good idea to read relevant books
and magazines about business and social etiquette. If in doubt, never be
afraid to ask for advice. Most people take it as a compliment, and unless you
feel you are going to lose face, it is usually the quickest way to get reliable,
up-to-date information.

MANNERS

Manners and etiquette are not quite the same thing. In her book *Modern
Etiquette*, Moyra Bremner aptly defines the difference thus: 'Etiquette
concerns the letter of the law, whereas manners are governed by its spirit.'
People with good manners treat others with courtesy, think of others before
themselves and have respect for each other.

Having good manners means behaving in a way that is socially acceptable, in business as well as domestic life. If we all followed the guidelines of good manners and mutual respect, we would treat each other more kindly, behave more honestly and enjoy both professional and social success.

ETIQUETTE

Standard etiquette usually reflects the manners and behaviour of a society's most successful group, which in Europe means the aristocracy and the professional classes. Etiquette has provided us with codes for behaving in a civilized fashion. Unfortunately, it has also supplied us with trivial rules that can be divisive, revealing which stratum of society we come from. Many of the more obscure codes of social behaviour are now obsolete, but there are some guidelines that still prevail. Whether or not you want to adhere to the rules, it is as well to know what the establishment regards as 'right'. To know how to behave in any society gives you enormous confidence, but it is important not to get so bogged down with the rights and wrongs that we cease to be ourselves or fail to enjoy a social evening, for example.

Codes of etiquette change over the years. At one time it was unthinkable for a gentleman not to offer his seat to a lady, open the door for her or carry heavy bags. I was talking to a young man recently who said that he would do no more for a woman than he would for any man. In these days of equality, there is nothing wrong with that, but good manners make a strong impression and they cost you nothing. It is polite to open a door for a male colleague and let him walk through first, so it is equally important to do the same for a woman. Physically, women do not find it as easy to stand for long periods compared to men, so it is thoughtful to offer a woman a seat on a long journey. Women are not as strong as men, so the offer of help with a heavy bag is usually welcome, just as it is with an elderly person of either sex. I realize, however, that some women do the rest of their sisters a disservice by seeing any offer of help as patronizing. It is a pity they are so insecure in themselves, but do not let that put you off! More and more women are beginning to realize what they will have lost if basic good manners disappear.

What is acceptable today was probably 'not quite the thing' a few years ago. The fact that more people use swear words these days does not make swearing any more acceptable. Keep your language as clean as possible, otherwise it will catch you out when you least expect it. Mine used to be rather colourful at times. I once uttered a rather choice word on live television after making a rather silly mistake – not something I ever wish to repeat. Coarse talk is just as bad as swearing, as it can create a very negative impression.

TABLE MANNERS

Being confronted by a glittering array of knives and forks can be quite daunting. It is all very well to heed the advice 'wait to see which one everybody else uses before you start', but what if you are the guest of honour and everybody is waiting for you? It is not easy to present a confident image if you use the fruit knife instead of the fish knife, or use a fork to eat asparagus when everyone else is using their fingers.

In my view, good table manners are essential. I am appalled by some of the very senior people I meet who can hardly hold a knife and fork, and eat in such a cumbersome way that it becomes distracting. If you spend a business lunch concentrating on whether your companion's food is actually going to make the mouth, rather than on what the person is saying, the whole episode can be counterproductive. Contracts have been won and lost on the tilt of a knife or the slurping of soup.

Our upbringing strongly influences our table manners. If children never sit down to a family meal, it not only deprives them of the chance to join in discussions involving the whole family, but it also denies them the opportunity to learn good table manners.

Handling Cutlery Correctly
Here are some guidelines for handling cutlery:

Tuck the handle of a knife into the heel of the right hand (if you are right-handed), with the index finger on top of it, pointing towards the blade. Do not hold the knife like a pen.
Hold the fork in a similar fashion, prongs towards the plate.
The soup and pudding spoons are held like a pen, but across the body and parallel to the table.

When used alone, the prongs of the fork face upwards, unless you are cutting food.

When you are not eating, put the utensils on the plate in a slight V shape, (to show that you have not finished). The handles should never rest on the table.

In Europe it is correct to use the knife and fork together, whereas in America the food is cut up with both implements, then the fork is put in the right hand to eat.

Keep your elbows close to your sides and hands low.

Lift food up to the mouth, rather than dipping the head to meet it.

It is not 'correct' to put a fork under the plate to enable the sauce to gather at one end.

Which Implement to Use When

The table is usually laid so that every implement, except the soup spoon and the bread or butter knife, has a partner, but you do not always use both. When confronted by a frightening array of silver, a good rule of thumb is to start at the outside and work your way in. This rule is not foolproof, however, as some people lay the bread or small knife on the side plate, some put it above the plate under the pudding spoon and fork and others place it to the left or right of the big knives. Do not be daunted if you make a mistake – either carry on eating with confidence (most people will not notice anyway) or acknowledge the fact that you always get confused and start again.

The classic way to set the table is thus:

On the Right

> Soup spoon on the outside.
> Next to it, the bread knife.
> Then the knife for the main course.
> Next to it, the pudding spoon.

On the Left

> The main-course fork on the outside.
> The pudding fork next to it.

Obviously, if you have more courses you will need more cutlery. Serrated knives are used only in restaurants, even for steak; but fish knives, which had been out of fashion for some time, are enjoying a comeback, except for oysters.

Tackling Tricky Food

With more and more foreign food now being eaten in this country, there are even more dishes to choose from and more decisions to be made on how to eat them. Here are some guidelines.

Rice and pasta should be eaten with a fork held in the right hand, prongs facing upwards.

Pâté is eaten only with a knife.

Puddings (sweets) should be eaten with both spoon and fork. A teaspoon should be used for puddings served in a glass or small bowl.

Asparagus is finger food and should only be eaten with a knife and fork when mixed with other vegetables. On its own, it should be held at the fat end, and the tips dipped into the sauce which has been poured onto the plate.

Globe artichokes are also finger food. If the middle leaves have been removed, the sauce goes in the hole, otherwise it goes on the plate. Pull off the outer leaves and dip the fleshy end into the sauce, biting hard enough to remove the flesh as you pull the leaf out of your mouth. Put discarded leaves on the plate provided, and when you reach the succulent base, eat it with a knife and fork.

Frog's legs are eaten with the fingers, as are spare ribs.

Game used to be the only meat that was eaten in the fingers, but now one uses a knife and fork for the sinewy legs, unless your host suggests otherwise.

Oysters and mussels should be lifted out of the shell with a fork (the French use a discarded mussel shell as a pair of pincers). Only the juice of an oyster should be drunk from a shell, otherwise use a soup spoon to finish any liquid. The empty shells should be put on the plate provided.

Snails are held by the shells with special tongs, and the snail twisted out with a sharp fork.

If prawns and shrimps are served in their shells, take off the head with your fingers and lift the shell away from the body before removing the tail. Once shelled, they are eaten with a knife and fork. Finger bowls as well as napkins should be provided. Incidentally, finger bowls should be filled with cold water, as this does not open the pores and allow odours to penetrate the skin.

A savoury soufflé is always eaten with a fork, whereas a sweet one is eaten with a spoon.

The correct way to consume soup is to push the spoon away from you as you scoop it up, and then sip it from the side of the spoon. In this country it is not done to lift or tip the bowl, unlike in Japan, where the bowl is lifted to the mouth.

Corn on the cob is rolled in butter and then bitten into carefully while holding it at each end with the fingers or special holders. Leaning your elbows on the table makes eating this rather unwieldy vegetable even less elegant!

Crab and lobster are rather a fiddle to eat unless the flesh has been dressed and put back into the shells. Larger claws have to be broken with a cracker and then the meat is scooped out with a lobster pick. For the smaller claws, use the fingers then eat the meat with a knife and fork. Brown bread and butter is served to be eaten with crab, not to have the meat spread on it. Both these shellfish can be rather messy to eat, so finger bowls and good-sized napkins are advisable.

Eat fish off the bone rather than fillet it on the plate. Remove the fine bones with your knife and fork and put them on one side. If you get one in your mouth, discreetly make a fist with your hand and deposit the bone into it before putting it on your plate.

Fruit can be a problem too. Oranges have been known to drench the person sitting next to you, and ripe mangoes will probably do the same to you. If in doubt – leave it out! On more formal occasions, fruit is halved with a knife and then eaten either with a knife and fork or with the fingers.

Cherry stones and grape pips are best dealt with in the same way as fish bones. Grapes should be cut or pulled off in small clusters. Melons and paw-paws are eaten with a spoon or a knife and fork, and kiwis should be cut in half and then eaten with a teaspoon.

In Britain it is correct to break bread rolls rather than cut them. When buttering, put the butter onto your plate first, and then apply to a small piece of bread at a time, rather than the whole piece. It is also polite to spread pâté, cheese or jams the same way.

Canapés and dips are very popular at drinks parties. When encouraged to 'have a little more', one is left in a quandary as to whether to remember the rules of basic hygiene or go ahead and dunk again. As Moyra Bremner says, 'follow the one dip per chip rule' or at least turn the crisp or piece of crudité round and use the unlicked end. Put used sausage sticks or olive stones onto an empty plate or, if there is nowhere else available, into your pocket (or your partner's)!

Salt should be poured onto the edge of the plate or taken with a spoon (even chips should be dipped into the salt and then eaten). Sea salt from a grinder is treated like pepper, which is sprinkled or ground over the food. Mustard and other sauces also go on the edge of the plate. It is slightly insulting to your host or hostess if you season the food before even tasting it, so try a little first. If it is not to your taste, as people are using less salt nowadays, make a light comment, such as you have always liked very seasoned food, even though you know it is not good for you.

Table Napkins

These are sometimes referred to as serviettes. Fabric ones are best, and they should be put across the knee and not used as a bib.

Wine

If you are going to have only one type of wine, then it should complement the main course and not be served until then. Some people, however, like to have a glass with every course including the pudding, and to accompany the cheese with port. If you are not sure what to order, ask the waiter what he or she would recommend. You can judge a good restaurant on the quality of the house wine. This is a good option if you are not sure which wine to choose, and it is not a particularly special evening. It is not a good idea to choose the second-cheapest on the menu, because that is usually the one on which the restaurant makes the most profit!

If the event is important, visit the restaurant beforehand and talk to the wine waiter. When entertaining at home, go to a good wine merchant and ask for advice based on what you are planning to eat. The wine may cost a little more, but it will be well worth it. Again, give yourself time to try the wine. However well recommended it is, do not buy something you do not like.

Glasses

An array of glasses can sometimes be a puzzle. There should be as many glasses as the number of drinks you will be offered. The tallest and slimmest glasses hold champagne, if it is to be served; the next tallest, tulip-shaped glass is for white wine, and the largest is for red wine. The smaller glasses are for sherry (with soup) or port. Tumblers are for spirits or water. No wine glass should be filled more than two-thirds full, as it swamps the bouquet. One tip: if you know you are likely to be drinking very good wine avoid wearing strong cologne or aftershave as it will mask the bouquet.

Sitting Down to Eat

When you are called to the table, either in a restaurant or a private house, do not linger to finish your drink or continue a fascinating conversation. The person who has been preparing the food will not be amused to see it spoil or go cold. If nobody makes a move, stand up and head gently for the door. For a formal meal, guests should not take their drinks with them (and it looks rude to gulp it down as if you are unsure whether or not you will get another), so leave what remains in the glass. During less formal evenings, your host will usually suggest you take the glass in with you. In a restaurant, a waiter will produce a tray to take drinks to the table.

Guests should wait to be seated by the host or hostess. If, however, they are told to sit where they like, it is usual to separate husbands and wives or partners, and for women and men to sit next to each other. Women sit first, but it is wise to wait a moment in case grace is said or any other ceremony observed. It is customary for the man to pull back the chair of the woman on his right. Unless you are quick, however, most women will seat themselves.

At a formal dinner the hostess usually starts off by talking to the person on her right, so follow her lead. The most important man sits on his hostess's right, and the next most important on her left. The most important woman sits on the host's right, and the next on his left. This is also the case for single-sex business dinners.

Smoking

It goes without saying these days that you should ask if you can smoke. It is embarrassing for both you and your hosts if they have to ask you to stop. If you are absolutely desperate for a cigarette, make an excuse to leave the room, have a few quick drags and return as quickly as you can.

Tipping

Tipping is entirely personal, but here are some general guidelines.

Ten per cent of the bill is the usual tip given to waiters (this also applies to taxi drivers and hairdressers). You can, of course, give what you like, and many people do. If service is included in the bill, do not feel you should have to give more unless the service has been exceptional.

The receiver of the tip appreciates knowing that you are pleased with the service rendered. I have asked many men and women in various lines of work about tipping, and they all say that the size of tip is not important, nor do they feel particularly offended if they do not get one. Nevertheless, tipping is expected in many areas.

What if you are invited to stay in a grand country house where tipping has always been part of the culture? Colin McBain is the butler at Burghley House in Lincolnshire. Although the house employs only a fraction of the staff it did at the turn of the century, the amount of entertaining is considerable, especially during the Burghley Horse Trials. After a stay in a country house you would expect to leave the butler £10 to £15, the same for the cook and another £10 for the maid. If the under-butler or chauffeur has been particularly helpful, you would tip them too. Colin says that if people do not give anything, he thinks nothing of it; however, most do. Single ladies do not leave a tip, but a single man does. In the case of couples, you tip the butler and other male servants while your partner sees to the female staff. You would leave the money in an envelope using the person's name, usually the Christian or first name.

Butlers and ladies' maids are very discreet, but their duties include unpacking for guests, so it is as well to bear that in mind! If you are shooting or fishing, you must also tip keepers, loaders and gillies. Ask your host for guidance as the amounts vary.

Complaints

If the service has not been good, then I will not leave a tip. Despite the emphasis on quality and customer care, there are still many places where the standards are not high, especially when the staff are young and the wages low.

It is important to say when you are not pleased with the way in which you have been treated, but you will get much further if you are courteous and well mannered. Having worked part-time in a hotel, I was surprised at the inconsiderate and often rude way I was treated. If you wish to complain to a waitress, you could try adapting the following examples:

'I am sorry, but the vegetables are cold. Do you think we could have some fresh ones?'
'I think this coffee has been sitting rather a long time. Would it be possible to have another cup?'
'We ordered some drinks a while ago now. Are they on their way?'

CORPORATE ENTERTAINING

Many companies still entertain their clients by inviting them to social, sporting and cultural events. While this should be great fun, do remember that you are there representing both yourself and your company, and therefore always 'on show'.

Flat Racing

This takes place in the summer. The most formal meetings are The Derby and Royal Ascot. If you are in the Royal Enclosure, morning dress with a top hat is the order of the day (black coat, grey waistcoat and grey striped trousers, or the 'Ascot Grey' morning suit). Otherwise a smart business suit is appropriate for this and other meetings. Many men wear trilbies, but hats are not obligatory. For Royal Ascot, a slip is usually sent with the vouchers mentioning points of etiquette. One to remember is that mobile phones are not allowed!

National Hunt Racing

The Grand National is the most famous meeting, followed by the Cheltenham Festival. As the weather is usually cold, a tweed suit is most suitable with a warm coat and a hat, but some men wear a pinstriped suit with a brown or black trilby. For a slightly more casual approach, jackets and cavalry twills fit the bill. If you are not in a box, a Barbour or waxed jacket and warm trousers will be fine.

Point-to-Point

These are races run by horses that have hunted. As far as dress goes, these are much more casual affairs. A tweed jacket, corduroy or cavalry twill trousers, green Hunter wellies and a Barbour will keep you warm and dry. A trilby is also a good idea, as well as an umbrella because the season runs from the end of February to late April.

Shooting and Fishing

You are unlikely to be asked to go game shooting unless you have shot before, but clay pigeon shoots are becoming increasingly popular. To tramp across the grouse moors you will need a warm shirt, a pullover, gloves, cap and a shooting suit. Alternatively, a pair of 'plus twos', thick socks to go inside wellingtons or shooting boots and a shooting coat or Barbour.

For a clay shoot, a Puffa or body warmer is worn over a jersey, trousers and walking shoes or boots. When the weather is cold, a cap is advisable, as are shooting gloves.

Salmon fishing can mean wading waist deep into icy streams, so a pair of waders is a must! Warm corduroy trousers, a jersey, a Barbour, gloves and green wellies will be needed if the weather is very cold. Some kind of headgear is advisable both for warmth and safety. A fly in the head can be a nasty experience, even more so if it is in the eye, so glasses are often worn for extra protection.

Shooting suits will cost anything from £300 and jackets from £150. Hunter wellies are priced around £50. Waxed jackets (of suitable strength and durability) cost between £80 and £100. Caps start at around £15, and sporting sweaters from £40. They are available at specialist gun shops and country sports shops.

Golf

If you are going to play golf seriously you need to be a member of a golf club and to buy proper equipment from specialist shops. When you are buying your clubs, you will be shown a wide range of clothes and shoes suitable for all seasons and at a range of prices. Most clubs do not allow jeans, shorts or T-shirts on the course, and some insist on a jacket and tie in the clubhouse. To be sure, take the appropriate attire with you.

Tennis

If you are invited to Centre Court or Number One Court at Wimbledon, cameras are not allowed. For other tennis tournaments, it is worth checking with your hosts if you are unsure of the rules.

Henley Regatta

Striped or plain blazers are worn for the Regatta, especially in the Members' Enclosure, and would be suitable in any of the hospitality tents.

Sailing

Hospitality sailing is usually a very social affair, and a trained crew is on hand to sail the boat. Most skippers are happy to show you the ropes if you fancy taking the helm, otherwise gin and tonics or hot rum are the order of the day.

For any sailing in this country, take warm trousers and sweaters as well as gloves and a waterproof jacket, as it can get very cold at sea. Soft-soled shoes are essential so that you do not mark the deck. Deck shoes or wellingtons are suitable, depending on the weather. If you are staying somewhere overnight, you will need more formal clothes as well.

Glyndebourne Opera

This is a summer event, and most people take a picnic that is eaten in the gardens if the weather is at all clement. Men usually wear dinner jackets, and it is prudent to take an overcoat and an umbrella, as well as a rug to sit on.

TITLES

It is awkward to be introduced to someone with a title, whether it is a noble or professional one, and not know how to address the person correctly. To have the information at your fingertips will give you the confidence to cope with even the most grand occasion. However egalitarian we might be, people still value a title if they have one, and so it is only polite to use it correctly. Here are some guidelines (example names are given in brackets):

The Queen is addressed as Your Majesty, and afterwards as Ma'am
(which rhymes with lamb).
The Duke of Edinburgh and The Prince of Wales are addressed as Your
Royal Highness and then Sir.
Other members of the royal family are addressed as Your Royal
Highness and afterwards as Ma'am or Sir.
Dukes and Duchesses – Your Grace.
Marquess or Marquis – Your Lordship, My Lord or Lord (Cholmondeley).
Marchioness – Your Ladyship or Lady (Cholmondeley).
Earl, Viscount and Baron – Your Lordship, My Lord or Lord (Rochester).
Their wives – Your Ladyship or Lady (Rochester).
Baronet – Sir (George).
His wife – My Lady, Your Ladyship or Lady (Carruthers).
Baroness – Lady (Thatcher).
Knight – Sir (Edward).
His wife – Lady (Flynn).
Dame – Dame (Judy).

Official Titles

Ambassadors – Your Excellency, Mr Ambassador or Ambassador.
Right Honourable Lord Mayors – My Lord Mayor or Lord Mayor.
Lord Mayors – as above.
Their wives – My Lady Mayoress or Lady Mayor.
Mayors – Your Worship, Mr Mayor or Mayor (Higgins).
Lord Provosts and Provosts – My Lord Provost, Provost, My Lord or Your
Lordship.
Aldermen and Councillors – Alderman (Jones), Councillor (Miller).

YOUR PUBLIC IMAGE ABROAD

It is useful to know something about other nations' habits in order
to judge our own in a healthier fashion, and not imagine everything
which differs from ours should be dismissed as ridiculous or
illogical, as is frequently done by those who haven't seen anything.

Descartes

It is vital to find out as much as you can about the country you are about to visit. Chambers of Commerce or the Trade Associations and Embassies of those countries will have information and guidelines, and are usually very helpful.

Tack Training International runs a series of training courses in Business Culture Training to help people who are trading abroad or want to move into joint ventures with foreign partners. Gerald McGregor is a director of Tack Training Worldwide. He explained to me: 'Cultures vary across nations and within nations. No culture is inherently superior or inferior, just different, and you need to be aware of these differences in order to be successful. Getting it wrong can lose you business.' A German politician once said on a visit to London: 'If I am selling to you I speak your language; if I am buying... dann müssen Sie Deutsch sprechen.'

Apart from learning the language of the country you propose to do business with, you must also master cultural differences in etiquette and manners. 'When you are at home you may argue about many things, and have widely differing views on both professional and personal matters, but you have many things in common,' says Gerald. 'But when you work overseas, or with people from different backgrounds, doing familiar jobs in unfamiliar circumstances can have a significant effect on the business itself.' Here are some examples:

In Hong Kong, the buyer may not get to know you personally and meet you for lunch or dinner until there is a good business reason for doing so.

In Japan, it is most impolite to sneeze or blow your nose in public (head for the nearest toilet).

In Spain, you would not do a deal unless the client felt he or she knew you well enough to trust you.

Southeast Asians judge a business person by their status and contacts.

In the Netherlands, time is a commodity that is allocated to specific purposes. At the end of the working day, the Dutch switch off and private life begins.

In the USA, the contract is what counts and the written word is all important.

In many Middle Eastern cultures, business discussions blend naturally

into personal conversation and family life. The spoken word is relied upon, and everything is renegotiable between friends.
British managers working in the Gulf should learn something about Islam, as religion infuses every aspect of life out there.

If you are not sure about gifts, just take something for the hostess. Nearly all women love presents, both in Britain and elsewhere. They do not have to be expensive as it really is the thought that counts. A bunch of flowers says a lot as a 'thank you'.

The following points of etiquette might be helpful when doing business in Europe.

France

Meals
In France, meals may be rather lavish and expensive. Breakfast meetings are very popular, and can be held in a café, your hotel or the firm's dining room. A business lunch can take up to three hours, and business should not be discussed until the coffee stage. The days of habitually long lunches are over, however, and a quick brasserie lunch is the norm for day-to-day dealings. Whoever issues the invitation pays the bill.

Gifts
If you are invited to someone's home, flowers or good chocolates are ideal for the hostess, and malt whisky or Cognac for the host. Never take wine in France. Corporate gifts such as pens are fine, but anything too expensive could cause offence.

Dress
Clothes should be fairly smart and classic, preferably a suit (as expensive as you can afford).

Belgium

Meals
Lunch is the most likely form of business entertaining, and the person who has issued the invitation pays. If you are asked to someone's home, it is a

real compliment. The Belgians entertain very lavishly, and if they take you out on the town, you will be treated to the best, which can take a long time as well as being expensive!

Gifts
Flowers are acceptable, but do not take alcohol. Modest corporate gifts are fine.

Dress
The Belgians dress rather conservatively. Spber suits are best, at least until you get to know your hosts.

Scandinavia

Although the guidelines below apply to Sweden, Norway, Denmark and Finland, there are cultural differences between these countries. When visiting a Scandinavian country, it is worth finding out as much as possible about its particular culture.

Meals
Breakfast meetings are popular, where the meal is substantial, but lunch hours are fairly short so you are most likely to be asked out for dinner. This could be at home or in a restaurant. If you eat at someone's house, it is important to phone and thank them the next day, (especially in Denmark).

Gifts
Flowers wrapped by the florist are popular, as are brandy or whisky.
A company gift should be well made and stylish.

Dress
The Scandinavians take a slightly more casual approach than the British.
A jacket and trousers would be fine.

Italy

Meals
If you are invited to lunch or dinner, you should accept; otherwise you might risk seeming uncivil. The meal will be a long-drawn-out and expensive affair,

and whoever issues the invitation usually pays. Let your host choose the restaurant, and bear in mind Italian time-keeping – do not make an appointment too soon after lunch!

Gifts

If you are invited to someone's home, take little presents for small children and flowers or chocolates. Corporate gifts should be of high quality and quite expensive.

Dress

Wear your most stylish suit, shirt and tie. Your shoes, in particular, should be as expensive as you can afford.

The Netherlands and Luxembourg

Meals

Breakfast meetings are not common, and lunch is unlikely to be a very ostentatious affair (perhaps even beer and a sandwich). Dinner is more relaxed, but not much business is discussed, as it is seen as a chance to get to know each other better. The person who issues the invitation pays. If you are invited to someone's home, it is a real compliment, so the hosts will appreciate a letter of thanks afterwards. Both these countries tend to be rather formal.

Gifts

Chocolates and flowers are acceptable gifts, but in the Netherlands they should cost at least £10 to £15. Wine can be agreeable in Luxembourg, but not in the Netherlands; if you are unsure, do not take it. From a company, the gift should be high quality but not too lavish.

Dress

Smart, conventional clothes are best. The Dutch are less formal than the British, but it would still be wise to wear a smart suit.

Spain and Portugal

Although I have grouped these two countries together, there are strong cultural differences within Spain itself, as well as with its neighbour.

Meals
Breakfast meetings are not very common, lunches and dinners being the norm. Spanish lunches are likely to be pretty lavish, and you will be expected to drink wine with your meal. A business dinner will usually start at ten or eleven at night, but after a lunch that has finished at five, you will not be too hungry! Being asked to someone's home is a very encouraging sign, and you will probably eat a little earlier.

The Portuguese, on the other hand, will not take offence if you do not want wine at lunchtime. You are quite likely to be invited to someone's home, or even away for the weekend, so a letter of thanks never goes amiss.

Both these countries are very hospitable and will want to pay for you, so let them if they insist.

Gifts
In Portugal, take chocolates and flowers for the host and hostess (except red carnations which remind the Portuguese of the revolution). The Spanish expect corporate, but not personal, gifts, so do some research into the company to find out what is acceptable.

Dress
A smart, stylish suit makes the best impression.

Greeting Business Partners

The question of the embrace as a 'hello' can be tricky. Take your lead from your host or hostess, both in Britain and the rest of the world. If the woman offers her cheek, give it a quick peck. Businessmen in most countries kiss both cheeks these days, but the Dutch kiss three times and some Frenchmen do four! The Russians sometimes kiss each other on the mouth (but they do not do this to foreigners unless they know them really well). Although the Japanese shake hands, they prefer to bow and exchange business cards. In Japan it is important to know the rank of the person you are dealing with, so make sure you have a nice wallet with large number of impressive business cards with you! This goes for any business meetings.

afterword

Brains and talent are merely the entry fee for the race. To win, you have to know the secret: Do unto others as you would have them do unto you.
Burt Manning, Chairman of J. Walter Thompson

In this age of 'win at all costs' it is wise to remember that what goes around, comes around. Honesty and integrity are part of projecting a confident and competent impression. Creating the right image means dealing with people in a polite and courteous manner. Truly respecting others provides the basis for motivation, and nobody is more persuasive than a good listener. Creating the right image means preparing in advance for meetings, interviews, projects and presentations. It means dressing with thought and style.

I do hope this book has been useful in helping you decide what your image should be, and has gone some way towards helping you achieve it!

bibliography

Bradley, Dinah. *Hyperventilation Syndrome: a Handbook for Bad Breathers*, Kyle Cathie Ltd, 1994

Brandreth, Giles. *The Complete Public Speaker*, Sheldon Press

Brandreth, Giles and Brown, Michele. *How to interview and be interviewed*, Sheldon Press, 1986

Bremner, Moyra. *Modern Etiquette*, Century Hutchinson Ltd., 1989

Carnegie, Dale and Ass. *The Leader In You*, Simon & Schuster, 1993

Gibbs, Paul. *Doing Business In The European Community*, Kogan Page Ltd., 1990

Hall, Nicola. *Principles of Reflexology*, Thorsons, 1996

Hopkins, Cathy. *Principles of Aromatherapy*, Thorsons, 1996

Hill, Richard. *We Europeans*, Europublications, 1993

Leith, James. *Ironing John*, Doubleday, 1995

Lindenfield, Gael. *Self Esteem*, Thorsons, 1995

Lyle, Jane. *Understanding Body Language*, Hamlyn, 1989

Maitland, Ian. *Answer The Question; Get The Job!*, Century Business, 1993

Mather, Diana. *Surviving The Media*, Thorsons, 1995

McCarthy, Margot (ed.). *Neals Yard Book of Natural Therapies*, Thorsons, 1994

Spillane, Mary. *The Complete Style Guide*, Piatkus

Spillane, Mary. *Presenting Yourself*, Piatkus, 1993
Summers, Vivian. *Public Speaking*, Penguin, 1988
Tannen, Deborah. *Talking From Nine to Five*, Virago, 1995
Tannen, Deborah. *You Just Don't Understand: Men and Women In Conversation*, Virago 1991
Velmans, Marianne and Litvinoff, Sarah. *Working Mother*, Corgi, 1993

index